THE SAND MAN

AN AUTOBIOGRAPHY

KARCH KIRALY

WITH

BYRON SHEWMAN

RENAISSANCE BOOKS

Los Angeles

Library of Congress Cataloging-in-Publication Data
Kiraly, Karch.
    The sand man / Karch Kiraly with Byron Shewman.
        p. cm.
    Includes index.
    ISBN 1-58063-054-5 (hardcover : alk. paper)
    1. Kiraly, Karch. 2. Volleyball players—United States—Biography.
    I. Shewman, Byron. II. Title.
GV1015.26.K57A3 1999
796.325'092—dc21
    [b]   99-10102
                                                CIP

10 9 8 7 6 5 4 3 2 1

Design by Lisa-Theresa Lenthall
Typesetting by Jesus Arellano

Distributed by St. Martin's Press
Manufactured in the United States of America
First Edition

CONTENTS

PREFACE

I've been ambivalent from the start of this project because I've never been fully convinced that the story of my volleyball career is one that needs to be memorialized in a book. Many people associated with my career strongly disagree, including Byron and our publisher. I've hesitated because: (1) Telling a story that's all about "me" (the definition of an autobiography) makes one sound so self-absorbed and self-indulgent, which distresses me because I try never to think or act that way in everyday life; (2) I haven't had to overcome abusive or neglectful parents or debilitating disease, but instead I've had all the advantages—parents, family, wife, kids, and friends who love and support me very much, the greatest teammates and coaches in the world—so I don't feel my career is all that compelling; (3) I can't look back and say I'm proud of my every action and it makes me uncomfortable to put myself under the microscope of hindsight; (4) Doing a project like this typically implies that an athlete's career has ended—mine has definitely not.

As you can see, everyone else won out so here you have it. Thank you so much for taking the time to judge for yourself.

—Karch Kiraly

ACKNOWLEDGMENTS

My co-author, Byron Shewman, and I would like to thank the following individuals for helping to make this book possible: Doug Avery and Peter Brouillet for their generous photo contributions; Jane Gelfman, the literary agent who believed in the project; and Jim Parish, the editor who donated much time and advice.

I'd like to acknowledge my parents, family, and friends for their unfailing support. I'd also like to thank every teammate and coach I've ever had the good fortune of working with for making our teams great and for making me better too. And, finally, I'd like to thank my wife, Janna, and our sons, Kristan and Kory, for making my life what it is today: beautiful.

CHAPTER ONE

LOOKING BACK...
AND AHEAD

Sitting next to my wife at dinner, my eyes went down the list of the one hundred athletes: Muhammad Ali, Bonnie Blair, Rafer Johnson, Jackie Joyner-Kersee, Oscar Robertson, Mark Spitz. Among them, the greatest boxer and showman the world had ever seen, and the swimmer who had captured seven gold medals in one single Olympics. What an awesome collection! They were all in this room together and even more incredible, I was counted as one of them.

I looked further at their individual accomplishments. Al Oerter, the great discus thrower, had won four gold medals in four straight Olympics. Only one other American athlete has matched that incomparable feat: Carl Lewis. Winning four gold medals is phenomenal in itself, but winning them over twelve years is even more of an accomplishment. The commitment to the daily regimen of preparing for a single Olympics is almost unimaginable—to continue that dedication for three more Olympics defies belief. Those particular names struck a distinct chord in me. Longevity was the attribute of which I was most proud in my own sports career.

Scanning that list of legendary athletes and their feats was the only moment when I ever questioned my decision to skip the Barcelona Olympics in 1992. Had I played, I might have had an opportunity to win four straight Olympic gold medals myself. But after being on gold-medalist teams in

1984 and 1988, I passed on the '92 Olympics for various reasons—reasons so strong that I never had a regret. Until that dinner.

Of course, the occasion had something to do with it. Tom Brokaw was the keynote speaker for the "One Hundred Golden Olympians," a gala evening held in Atlanta, Georgia, the night before Opening Ceremonies of the 1996 Olympics. Attended by such luminaries as IOC (International Olympic Committee) president Juan Antonio Samaranch, many of America's greatest living sports legends were being honored. Criteria for selection in the group included winning at least one Olympic gold medal and serving as an exceptional role model. Only six honorees at the dinner were actually competing in Atlanta. Carl Lewis and Jackie Joyner-Kersee were two of them. I was another.

Within a few weeks I would be shooting for a third gold medal. This time it would be in beach volleyball, newly accepted into the Olympic games. When I hung up my indoor shoes in 1992, I never imagined that the beach version of the sport would be in the Olympics. But here it was. I knew my partner, Kent Steffes, and I had a good chance to win it—we had dominated the AVP (Association of Volleyball Professionals) tour the past five years.

Somewhere in the back of my mind that potential fourth gold medal was still shining, although dimly. If we could win in Atlanta—maybe, just maybe—I could hold on until the 2000 Olympics and win a fourth gold. To win in 2000 would mean being the best in the world at age thirty-nine. That was an intimidating thought. Later, I would also find out that a fourth gold medal in Sydney 2000 would represent something never before done in Olympic history: four gold medals over a *sixteen-year* period.

The notion didn't linger long. I had enough on my hands—and mind— just to win a third gold in Atlanta.

As the 1995 AVP season was winding down, the summer was also ending. Yet, there was an uncharacteristic energy in the air—a sense of new beginnings. Beach volleyball, spawned on the sands of Santa Monica in 1930 and remaining a Southern California cult game for some half century, had just gotten the ultimate blessing of sport legitimacy. It would be included in the 1996 Olympics in Atlanta.

The quest for Olympic status was led by Ruben Acosta, president of the FIVB (Federation Internationale de Volleyball). On one hand, we were thrilled with his efforts. On the other, we resented his designs to control the sport of beach volleyball—particularly on American soil, or so we perceived it as such. In the end, the good outweighed the bad. Sure, our new Olympic rings were entangled in politics and power plays, but we had finally arrived. The game we loved so much was going to be played on the world's center stage.

For me, Atlanta took on special meaning. Beginning with my college career at UCLA, I had spent over a decade largely devoted to indoor volleyball, reaching the pinnacle of that sport on the world level. Great as that was, there was a constant, gnawing pain with which I had to live. It came from loving both versions of my sport—indoor and beach volleyball—and the fact that until 1992 I could only play on the sand part-time. Although I stayed close to the top level on the beach—during the partial seasons I played—I couldn't find a partner with whom I could consistently win. The problem was simple. To play on the USA Men's Team required most of my time. In fact, I had not competed in a full beach season since high school.

By 1992 I was dying to get back to where I played my first game at age nine. I'd been away long enough from the sun, the sand, the ocean, the California dream I loved so much. I now had a wife and two young sons, and a house in San Clemente. Tired of the nonstop traveling and playing in hundreds of gyms around the world, I was ready for the beach. So was my family.

In 1991 I had finally hooked up with my longed-for ideal partner, Kent Steffes. We quickly shot to the top of the beach game, then stayed there. Still, the '96 Olympics was the big one—for our sport and for me. Kent and I wanted to grab the biggest prize of all and I decided to be as ready for that Olympic contest as anything I'd ever prepared for in my life.

During the year leading up to Atlanta, I applied a precept to my already strict daily routine. It was simple: I never wanted to look back after Atlanta and say that I hadn't made my maximum effort every day to be totally ready for victory.

In the end it worked. Kent and I were able to come away with the first Olympic gold medals for beach volleyball draped around our necks. The media coverage at "Atlanta Beach" was remarkable—the event was viewed as "the most cool" place to be in the Games. Within days, Kent and I were on the Jay Leno show. Indeed, it looked like our fledgling game was poised to storm the beaches of the world.

How wrong we were. Unbeknownst to us AVP players, our organization was already teetering on financial collapse. Financial mismanagement coupled with the failure of the board of directors—made up of players—to hold management's feet to the fire hard enough had pushed our pro tour to the brink of disaster.

The AVP's sudden woes seemed to parallel my own. I suffered the first serious physical setback of my life—one that almost ended my playing career—only weeks after the Atlanta Olympics. Years of wear and tear on my shoulder ended with a severely torn rotator cuff that put me under the surgeon's knife, followed by a long and frustrating rehabilitation period. In the summer of 1997 I would begin losing to opponents whom I normally waxed on the court. My partner, Kent Steffes, eventually dropped me for another partner and I would have to wrestle with grave self-doubts about my chances to get back to where I once was in the sport.

As if things weren't bad enough for me on the sand, I somehow got sucked into the financial debacle of the AVP—much against my wishes. It would culminate in rancorous lawsuits, including one filed against me by my former Olympic partner.

I watched in pain as the AVP slowly began to sink—TV ratings fell steadily, as did prize money—while old friendships and relationships were sundered amid nasty recriminations at every turn. Perhaps the biggest blow came when Miller Brewing decided not to renew its title sponsorship at the end of the '98 season.

It had been a hard time and unexpected. Fully aware that the challenges would only increase, I knew that I had to keep looking at the big picture. Above all, I had to focus on the fact that I still loved playing the game after so many years. I was able to do that. At the end of the '97 season, my efforts to rehab my shoulder finally bore fruit and my new partner, Adam Johnson, and I were able to claw our way to the top level of the tour.

During the 1998 AVP season, Adam and I continued on our upward swing—winning six tournaments during the season, including the last three that we competed in. Then, two events prior to the season's end, Adam came down with a back injury that knocked us out of those final competitions.

Still, I was thrilled with our season and my own level of play. I had now racked up 136 Open wins—only three away from tying Sinjin Smith's all-time record. That would serve as an added motivation for the upcoming year.

And even more exciting, Sydney 2000—and possible Olympic history for me—was not terribly far away. The key was to keep my eye on what had always been most important. Playing.

CHAPTER TWO

EAST BEACH

East Beach in Santa Barbara, California, is the most beautiful place in the world to play volleyball. And my summers during high school, in the mid-1970s, were the most fun times I ever had in the sport. My buddies and I would race our bikes down in the morning to see who got there first. Usually it was me or John Hanley, who would later become a great pro beach player.

East Beach was breathtaking. It still is despite a few changes and the fact that many more people go to the beach there. Back then, there was a gorgeous grassy area with huge, towering pine trees. You could sit on the grass and look out at the white sand where the courts were always impeccably maintained by the city. Farther out was the Pacific Ocean, sparkling in the sun, and behind you like an emerald backdrop were the Santa Barbara Mountains.

On the grass there were so many different things going on. All the regulars—Rich Riffero, Jerry Evans, Tully Ramsaur, Bill Conway—the guys who had been going there for years would show up midmorning. Since they were older, in their thirties and forties, they weren't the best players but everyone knew and respected them. They'd play a little, then play some cards, then play another game, then play more cards. We kids just played volleyball. We deferred to them and they directed who played on what court and when. There were a half-dozen courts in those days but the most important was the A court. The *gods* came down to the A court—mostly guys from University of California, Santa Barbara—who were some of the best players in the nation.

There were always pretty girls, typical California beach beauties. Especially when girls from our high school came down, we seemed to play a little harder.

Paradise. Except for one problem—the wind. Local players were so spoiled by the pristine conditions at East Beach that when the wind picked up out of the west in the afternoon, they would knock off volleyball and turn to playing cards: hearts, gin rummy, funiente, sometimes bridge. The wind never stopped Hanley and me. Maybe it wasn't as much fun with the ball blowing around but we got more games in. Then about six in the afternoon the wind calmed and it would be awesome down there. Breathless. Just the right temperature, seventy-five degrees, and since most of the beach was empty by then, we could get even more playing time. After the last game we'd jump in the ocean, about seven o'clock, then go around the corner to Tri-Counties Fruit and get a big watermelon to break open. In front of an incredible red and gold sunset spread out before us, we'd sit. Sunbaked, dried salt in our hair, exhausted. The best feeling was that we knew we'd outlasted everybody on the beach. Even the grown men—we wore them down too. Life couldn't get any better.

Outlasting the other guys gives me the same thrill today. Most of the wins on the AVP tour that I cherish most are the times we've come through the losers' bracket. To do that you have to play seven games on Sunday, without cramping, pushing your body when there's not much left to go on.

In high school I usually teamed with Hanley. He played the right side and I played the left exclusively—I grew up playing that side because my dad played the right. Usually the first two kids at the beach, John and I would start peppering the ball back and forth. "Pepper" is volleyball jargon for the exercise of two players warming up with the ball. You simply face your partner, about fifteen feet apart, then set, hit, and dig the ball back and forth. We would play pepper until two other regulars showed up and the first game of the day got under way. What evolved was a contest between John and me over who could get in the most games in a day.

"How many did you get today?" we'd ask each other at sunset. The best way to increase that number was to keep winning. "Winners" is a system where the winning team stays on the court until beaten by another team. So you had to get there early and stay on the court, because if you lost you'd have to wait some games to get back on and challenge the winning team.

Hanley had the record. Thirteen straight wins—on the court from nine in the morning until seven at night. He could have won a few more that day but everyone had finally gone home. The most I ever got was nine. Nine means a lot of playing, but thirteen is outrageous.

We played so much and got so good so fast. To see ourselves improving almost daily, spending our summers doing what we loved to do, was a dream. Plus, playing all those hours in the sand gave us legs of steel and did wonders for our body control.

Those were the glory years of UC Santa Barbara. Great indoor players and some were top beach players as well: Gary Hooper, Jon Roberts, Jay Hanseth, Don Shaw, Skip Allen, Gerald Gregory. Of course, they played on the A court near the grass while we got the courts on the periphery.

Finally one day we mustered the nerve to try to call "winners" on the A court. The older guys just scoffed at us: "Get serious, punks! Get outta here!" We were only fifteen, so the rejection didn't bother us. We stayed on the lower courts and kept getting better. And we kept asking.

After enough pestering, one late afternoon the top players finally let us on the A court. They hammered us 15–1 or 15–2, but after a month or so it was more like 15–7. By the end of summer they had to work their butts off to beat us. What a feeling! The best college players in the nation were groveling to beat some fifteen-year-old kids.

My parents, Toni and Las, fell in love with Santa Barbara the first moment they saw it. They decided that's where we would settle one day—even though it would take several years to get there. My dad's not a man to be denied.

The first time we saw it was in the summer of 1966, just after my dad finished his junior year of medical school at the University of Michigan. He and my mom wanted to come out to California, like a lot of people in Michigan, for his year of internship. We visited some hospitals in Los Angeles and were on our way to see more in San Francisco, when we made a short, but planned, visit to the little town of Santa Barbara. After driving along the beach, looking at the mountains, and seeing a few sights, my dad moved Santa Barbara straight to the top of his request list. He got in.

My dad has quite a history of getting what he wants—through sheer determination if nothing else. He was born in north Hungary in 1935. I remember him telling me about one summer when he and a few buddies lugged a lot of heavy equipment around to survey the desolate Hungarian *puszta* (plains). He was studying to be an engineer then and they had to survey territory that no one even occupied. A typical Communist job, I guess. His first love since childhood was medicine, but because his father had a small business making leather transmission belts for small motors, with one employee under him, he was considered a bourgeois by the local Communist party. That meant losing certain privileges, including his son getting into medical school.

"We want the sons of peasants and workers to be our doctors and architects," my grandfather was told. My dad's top-notch grades didn't count for med school under the Communist regime. So he had to settle for engineering.

When the Soviets invaded Hungary in 1956, my dad was just twenty-one and a university student. It didn't take long before he became a freedom fighter during that uprising, tossing Molotov cocktails at Soviet tanks—like a lot of his friends—and running for freedom. He had a Soviet-made machine gun under his jacket when he finally made it to the Austrian border, crawling on his belly through all kinds of abandoned fields. After tossing the gun away, in the dead of night under Soviet rockets lighting up the sky, he crossed into Austria on his hands and knees.

"I kissed the ground," he later told me.

He had seen what was going to be the end result of the invasion earlier than most and decided that he couldn't stand living under those conditions—without his freedom. He had a five-year-old sister, Gabi, and he told me that the hardest thing about escaping was leaving her. Today she runs a beauty and fitness parlor out of her home in Budapest and they have remained close.

So, with a bag of clothes over his shoulder, he took a U.S. Army boat across the Atlantic and ended up in a refugee camp in New Jersey. On a bulletin board in a Lutheran church he saw an announcement offering a $500 scholarship for a Hungarian student, at the University of Michigan. He won it and, through washing dishes at a fraternity house, worked his way through school and obtained a master's degree in engineering. In college he met my mom, Toni, who had come from upstate New York to attend Michigan also.

I was born Charles Frederick Kiraly on November 3, 1960, in Jackson, Michigan, which is not too far from Ann Arbor. After my birth, my mom went on to get a master's degree in library science at the University of Michigan, then later worked as a school librarian and taught elementary school in Ann Arbor. After getting his master's degree, my dad went to work as a civil engineer, but after a couple of years he found it too boring—maybe he'd done too much surveying during his teenage summers back in Hungary. However, the real reason was his first love: medicine. After several weeks of consideration, he and my mom decided he would go back to school to become a doctor.

I was a happy kid in Ann Arbor, in Little League and Boy Scouts, and playing with my friends. So happy that the only trauma I faced happened every year on the first day of school—before the whole class I'd have to explain to the teacher not to call me Charles, but to use my nickname, Karcsi (which means Chuck) Kiraly (which means king). Of course, it was Hungarian and pronounced "KARCH-ee" and "KEER-eye" but my buddies would be snickering as I went through the exercise year after year. I was called Karcsi until sometime during college when people started calling me Karch more often. About that time I decided to make things easier and change my name to Charles Karch Kiraly (which is redundant), though I continued to go by Karch.

I was six when we moved out to Santa Barbara in 1967 for my dad's internship year of medicine. He and his doctors-to-be friends found an apartment complex on Bath Street. It had a swimming pool. Cottage Hospital was just up the street. As interns, they were all quite young, married, and most had kids. Since their children were already my friends, moving wasn't too traumatic for me. My dad and his colleagues worked their tails off during the week, but they let loose on Friday night with loud music and dancing by the pool. Rumor went that my dad was dancing so hard one evening that his watch flew off and into the pool. That's energy. About nine o'clock one of my parents would usually say, "Karcsi, why don't you go up and watch *Star Trek*."

On Saturdays and Sundays all the families would go to the beach. I remember that my dad was in heaven. He had played on the Hungarian Junior National Volleyball Team as a teenager and later played in Michigan whenever he could, on indoor teams and on the lakeshores during summers. However, he had never played beach doubles. That summer he saw his first Open beach tournament—the 1967 Santa Barbara Open—which was always held around July 4. Ron Lang and Ron Von Hagen, two of the greatest beach players ever, were practically unbeatable at the time and won it. My dad was just blown away by the game and the whole atmosphere. He was hooked. He still plays every day—sixty-three and in great shape.

My dad started me playing that summer. "Put your thumbs together, lock your elbows, and bump the ball off your forearms." Unless you've tried it, you don't realize how awkward it feels when you begin bumping. Setting a volleyball is a strange sensation at first too—taking the ball with your cupped hands before flicking it out with your fingers. It's so foreign compared with other sports where you're taught to catch the ball and hold onto it. Volleyball skills take time and I was lucky to learn them at such a young age.

My mom still has home movies of me—a skinny, little towhead—and my dad bumping the ball back and forth. But I don't remember much of that. I was more into just being a kid—digging huge holes in the sand where my friends and I could hide from one another, swimming, jumping in the waves, building sand castles.

The beach is the best place in the world for a kid. Today when I look at my own kids frolicking there, I sometimes see myself. Building sand castles, throwing rocks at the waves, climbing up in the lifeguard tower, throwing volleyballs into the net, they entertain themselves. My parents never had to worry about me when I was at the beach. It's a place where kids can expend all of their energy in a positive way.

My mom recalls that when I was about ten my dad had a tendency to push me to play when I didn't feel like it or when I was tired. I don't remember it that way. My memories of early playing are that it was pure fun. It still is, which is why I'm still able to play with such enthusiasm.

The other big reason that I loved the beach game so much was the thrill, at eleven or twelve years old, of doing what grown men could do. The primary strategy in beach doubles is to find and exploit the weaknesses in either of your opponents. Obviously, they went after the kid and they tried to serve me every ball. At that age I couldn't hit a ball downward—the net was too high—but I could use control shots that were just as valuable.

Control shots are valuable in beach volleyball because stamina is such a big part of the game. Unlike tennis, points are scored only when you serve. So if my opponent is serving and we break his serve—or "sideout"—then the serve reverts to our team and we have a chance to score. With siding-out, a lot of playing can go on without points being scored.

As far as control shots, I had a dink, which is the short shot just over the net. I had a cut, which travels along the net and lands near the far sideline. I also had a deep line and a deep angle shot, both placements in the opponents' deep corners. Once I had enough control, it gave me great pleasure to frustrate grown men by just mixing up my shots and hitting the four corners of the court. The bottom line is that I was good at it and it was fun to keep getting better.

Even at that early age I played for the joy of it, which I believe is the real reason why you should do anything—for your own enjoyment. Not long ago I was preparing a speech to deliver to the USA Ski Team, and in searching for a quote about success I stumbled upon this one by Ernest Hemingway: "It's enough for you to do it once for a few men to remember you. But if you do it year after year, then many people remember you and they tell it to their children, and their children and grandchildren remember and, if it concerns books, they can read them. And if it's good enough, it will last as long as there are human beings."

It struck me that he was doing it—in this case, writing—for everybody else. That's not me at all. I don't play for people to recognize me, or remember me, or to please anybody else. I do it for me. I take great pride in being prepared and competing well, and I'm not overly concerned with other people's opinions. Most of the time they have nice things to say, but I try not to listen to that either because I've learned—especially playing in the Italian pro league after my USA Team career—that those nice comments can be very ephemeral. So I play for my own satisfaction, rather than to be remembered by people who don't really know who I am.

After that year of paradise in 1967, we moved back to Ann Arbor for my dad's residency, which lasted three years. During that time he played on an indoor team for the Ann Arbor YMCA. Since he was so busy during the week, the only chance I had to be with him was the weekends. We would wake up at three or four on Saturday morning, meet his teammates somewhere, and drive all over the Midwest on icy winter roads—Grand Rapids, Flint, Chicago—for USVBA tournaments. I was usually the only kid at the tournaments, spending much of the day by myself. If my dad or one of his teammates wasn't totally exhausted, sometimes they'd play pepper with me. Or I'd run on those overhanging tracks that the older YMCA gyms had, or shoot at an empty basketball hoop. Those tournaments started at nine in the morning and could end past midnight. Many times I'd be asleep on the bleachers when they were over. But I learned about being independent and how to entertain myself.

That's one thing I like so much about the beach—I control my own destiny. I'm my own coach. Recently I heard Jerry West, the basketball legend, talking about the same thing. After playing so many years of a team sport, he turned to golf after his retirement. And he really liked the individual aspect of the game. What you put into it, you get out of it.

On the beach I see much more direct results of my efforts—including prize money. You have a partner but it's a far cry from the twelve players, plus coaches, on an indoor volleyball team. I set a precise training program for myself and I take it seriously.

Not that I didn't enjoy playing indoor as well. In particular, I liked the international competition. I knew we were playing against the best in the world and I loved taking a guy's best shot. If I could stand in and dig his hardest hit, or even cover and save a ball for my teammates, we had the guys who could finish the play. I liked being the initiator. Steve Timmons and Pat Powers were the terminators. When a ball was dug and put up for one of them, a point was almost automatic. That was the formula that made us the best team on the planet.

My dad couldn't wait to be done with his residency and get back to Santa Barbara. But at that time, there wasn't an opening there for his specialty—physical rehabilitation. Although we did manage to get back to California in 1971, it was first to Saratoga (near San Jose) for a year, then to Claremont, which is a smoggy inland town about twenty miles east of Los Angeles. By that time I was really into soccer. My dad had played that too, and since there was no organized volleyball for kids in Michigan, it was natural for me to turn to soccer. My dad usually coached the teams I was on and I was pretty good, but he still bumped the volleyball with me on a regular basis.

A year before my dad finished his residency in Michigan, we took a summer vacation in Santa Barbara and I played my first volleyball game. I was nine. I remember that I played against my dad and local legend Bill Conway, who was affectionately known as the "mayor" of East Beach. To even it out they gave me a pretty good player whom they'd nicknamed Jack the Rat. I think we lost, but I still remember the thrill of playing my first real game.

East Beach is such a big part of me. My first taste of volleyball at six. My first game at nine. Little did I know what other great things lay ahead for me on that beautiful stretch of white sand.

CHAPTER THREE

RISE AND HIT!

When I was about nine, I read a *Sports Illustrated* article about Larry Rundle, the great UCLA player, and it stated that he had been the youngest player ever to compete in an officially sanctioned beach tournament. I wanted to beat that record. I actually tied it in 1972, playing with my dad in my first tournament—a novice tournament—at Corona Del Mar in Orange County, California. I was eleven. It was the only time I ever went out of a tournament with two straight losses, but the games were really close. Above all, I was competing against grownups in a real tournament.

For the next four summers in California, my dad and I played in a lot of tournaments. In 1974 we moved back to Santa Barbara, and that move cemented my lifelong commitment to volleyball. Soccer would soon be a thing of the past.

My dad was my only partner until I was fifteen. We competed in novice and B tournaments because at the time I wasn't a very strong player. Too young, too small. But I got better every year and in 1976 my dad and I finally earned our B rating in a tournament at Muscle Beach in Santa Monica. For a fifteen-year-old that was a major milestone.

In the early days beach volleyball status was determined by a rating system—one that had been established in the 1960s under the guidance of the Santa Monica Recreation Department. The lowest level of competition was novice, or unrated. Players advanced from novice, to B, to A, to AA, and finally to the top rating of AAA. For example, to achieve a AAA rating, a player had to win a AA tournament or finish fourth or higher in a AAA tournament. Tournaments were held only on weekends—from Santa Barbara down to San Diego.

Every summer the Santa Barbara Open was held at East Beach. In 1975 John Hanley and I went down to watch the tournament. One of the top teams was Ron Von Hagen and Tom Chamales. Von Hagen was an awesome player. He had a sculptured body rippling with muscles and looked like a Greek god. In 1996 Von Hagen was ranked by *Volleyball Magazine* as the second-best beach player of the sport's fifty-year history. But in 1975 he was thirty-five and close to retirement. Chamales was much younger and also a physical phenom. One of my most vivid memories is a play in which Chamales hit the ball so hard that it bounced almost as high as the trees—about twenty-five feet—and that's not easy to do on the beach. It was the most awesome thing we'd ever seen. Hanley and I looked at each other stupefied, but even stranger for us was that the guys on the court didn't even flinch. They seemed to shrug their shoulders and say, "That's just what this guy does."

How high you can bounce a volleyball has always been a test of machismo in this sport—a combination of jumping ability and a fast arm. It's a particularly big deal in warm-ups. I was a horrible warm-up hitter. One reason is that I always practiced hitting the ball flat and deep in the court. For me it was more important to think about hitting against a block and beating it. During my career on the USA Team, when we dominated the world between 1984 and 1989, we always lost the warm-ups but usually won the game.

I try to control my game, which is probably a result of my upbringing. I grew up in a pretty disciplined household, where hard work was emphasized. I think it was that old-world ethic, where instead of complaining a lot about your problems you just work harder to make them better. Of course, my dad was a paragon of that idea.

But it was primarily our mom who raised us. She was the nurturer. As hard as it is to work eighty to ninety hours a week as an intern, it's not like a twenty-four-hour-a-day job in which you're the main parent bringing up children. That's the hardest and most important job of all. My mom was also good at juggling five things at once, and that means you can't do any of them perfectly.

I've learned that instead of striving for perfection, efficiency, and firmness—my father's strengths—parenting requires you to tolerate errors and chaos, to accept your kids' unique and individual development, and to be as gentle and spontaneous as possible every day. In helping to form a human being, sometimes discipline and regimen don't fit. You can't say that today my kid is going to learn to tie his shoes, because kids develop on their own timetable no matter how much you might want their progress to work on yours. You have to be prepared for setbacks and surprises, things that are out of your control.

I have two sisters, Kati and Kristi, who are seven and twelve years younger than I. My dad spent more time with me—because I was a boy and because of our shared soccer and volleyball activities. My sisters were into horses, which he knew nothing about, so he obviously related better to me than to them.

My younger sister, Kristi, played volleyball one year in high school but the coach kept comparing her with me and that ruined her experience. She quit and never played volleyball again. Being held up to someone else's standard is something no one needs—especially not a sibling, a child, or any other family member. And that's the reason why at home I downplay evidence of my accomplishments, so as not to burden my kids or my wife. People are sometimes shocked that I don't have a trophy room in our house.

I only want my kids to play volleyball if it's their own choice. If they pursue other interests, that's fine. There's been enough volleyball in my life to suffice for my entire family. In fact, during much of my life, my commitment to the sport left me too little time for others. I love my sisters very much, but we lead quite separate lives. Kristi works for DKNY in New York City and Kati now lives in Santa Barbara, traveling frequently for a medical manufacturing company.

I consider myself very fortunate. As a child I received beneficial—although very different—things from both my parents. My dad was continually buzzing with energy and he had a history of starting and developing things. One thing he started was the Santa Barbara Blues Society to bring in blues performers from all over the country. What I admire most about him is his ability to organize his life, especially how prepared he is to face whatever might confront him—the next day, the next week, the next year. Whether it's his job or a competition, he maximizes his preparation so that nothing can surprise him.

"Rise and hit!" is a saying—with a tinge of Hungarian accent—made famous by my dad at East Beach. Anyone happening by the Santa Barbara shore during the last twenty years would probably have heard my dad before seeing him. Not surprisingly, I was a pretty quiet player as a kid, likely because he did all the talking and yelling. Normally it didn't bother me, but I remember one time either asking him or telling him not to yell quite so much during a tournament in Santa Barbara. My buddies were watching and I must have felt it wasn't cool to be playing with your dad, especially when he's yelling his head off. To be fourteen or fifteen and spending so much time with your father, while most kids are rebelling at that age, made it hard sometimes. Today I realize it's just his boundless passion and enthusiasm for the game and that shouldn't be stifled at all.

I shared my dad's driving nature, although on a quieter level. His outgoing manner probably made me turn more inward, but the hard edge of competitiveness was still there. After spending a lot of time with my wife, Janna, and then having kids, I learned about my softer side. And I think it's made me a better person and a better volleyball player. In the early days I tended to define myself strictly by what happened on the volleyball court. If we lost a tournament or big match, I sometimes felt that my whole week was ruined. I'd be down; my self-esteem would suffer. I wasn't Karch—husband and dad—I was just a volleyball player. But for a long time now I've known that my wife and children are far more important to me than a game could ever be.

"Apu, what should I do?" I asked my dad, addressing him with the Hungarian word for father that I always used.

It wasn't an easy question I was asking him. He was the only partner I'd ever had, and now I was thinking about playing with someone else for the first time.

That was in 1976 and the occasion was the upcoming Santa Barbara Open. As always, it livened things up at East Beach because the best players in the sport were coming to town. Although I was only fifteen and had never played in an Open, I was becoming known around East Beach as a kid with promise. A few weeks before the tournament a good local player, Rich Payne, came up and asked me to play in the event. I didn't know what to say, except, "I gotta talk to my dad."

My father gave me a straight answer. "I think you should play with him. It won't hurt my feelings. You're already better than I am and you're gonna get a lot better. You might as well start now."

So Rich and I practiced for a day or two. On the Saturday morning of the Open all my friends came down to the beach to watch. One of the first teams we played was Jon Lee and Curt Donaldson, whom we ended up beating. Jon was a good local player and brother of Greg Lee, a UCLA basketball player who won a lot of beach Opens with Jim Menges. My dad was watching, very excited. At one point he heard Jon say, "I can't believe I'm losing to a fifteen-year-old kid!"

That wasn't the only time the line was heard that day. In the next game we faced Jeff Jordan and Leonard Armato. Leonard would later play a major role in the AVP as its first executive director and, of course, today he is a top sports agent with clients such as Shaquille O'Neal. Law school probably helped Leonard exert self-control—something Jeff Jordan wasn't good at. By now the East Beach locals were in force on the sidelines in their beach chairs and really pulling for us. As we increased our lead, Jordan got more flustered and tried to unravel me verbally, trying to humiliate me. Finally he just lost his mind and started screaming obscenities. I remember being astounded how a grown man could entirely lose his composure because he was losing to a teenager. But we won, and all of a sudden we were facing Menges and Lee in the quarterfinals of the tournament.

Menges and Lee had never seen me, so they thought, "Let's serve the kid." Since Rich was a good setter, I was able to get into a good hitting rhythm. Menges and Lee were having trouble scoring points. Finally they quit serving me and I think that caught both Rich and me off guard. Rich was so shocked that he made some hitting errors and they beat us two straight games. But it took a long time. We made it to Sunday morning, though we lost our first match that day. Making it to Sunday has always been a benchmark for aspiring players, and getting there in my first Open—against the best players in the world—was a big thrill. We finished ninth and that earned me an A rating.

Funnily enough, my dad played in a B tournament in Santa Barbara about a month later with his own new partner and won it, making him an A-rated player also. One Saturday morning soon after, on my way to work at a falafel stand, I rode my bike down to East Beach to see the start of the local A tournament. Since I had to work, I couldn't play. I noticed this guy pacing nervously because his partner hadn't shown up. He asked me to play. Marco Ortega was a strong player, three or four years older than I, and this seemed like a good opportunity. I called in to work and got someone to replace me.

"Guess who our first game is against?" Marco asked me.

"Who?"

"Your dad!"

I'll never forget it. How different it was now to be on the other side of the net from him. Neither of us wanted to lose and it turned into a real dog fight, our toughest match of the tournament. We went on to win it 15–13 and I got my AA rating at fifteen years old—an accomplishment I was very proud of. For players in those days, the rating was what determined prestige. You could win a trophy, but getting another A added to your rating meant much more.

The summer of 1976 was a huge one for another reason—the Olympics. My friends and I had been reading *Volleyball Magazine,* so we already knew of the top players who would compete in Montreal. We used to sit around until one of us would pretend to be a world all-star and start talking trash, "All right, I'm Alexander Savin of Russia—six feet seven inches, with a forty-two-inch jump, and I can put any hitter in a telephone booth."

Another guy would say, "Big deal! I'm Diego Lopera of Cuba. My vertical is fifty inches and I can go over any block." We'd get so fired up, we'd have to jump on our bikes and pedal down to the gym. Hanley and I were pretty good at sneaking into gyms, so we'd get in, put up a net, and play until a janitor happened by. Sometimes they'd boot us out; the nicer ones let us stay.

We had already seen some world-class foreign players in Santa Barbara. In 1975 a pro league, the IVA (International Volleyball Association) was started with a handful of teams, mostly in Southern California, and Santa Barbara had a franchise. The league's owners felt that the sport needed more entertainment, so they imported some top foreign players. They also made it a coed format: four guys and two women who played only in the back court. To us kids it seemed bizarre to see mixed teams, but the good thing was that we got a chance to see some awesome players.

Wilt Chamberlain, the great basketball player, was part of that league. He liked to play volleyball and was such a huge name in sports that the league thought he could attract television interest for the sport. At seven feet one inch, his hitting was impressive but the rest of his game was pretty rough.

Of the great foreigners, the most amazing was Stan Gosciniak from Poland—selected as the MVP of the World Championships in 1974. He was like a cat. He'd throw his body around the court—dive from any position, get the ball up, and somehow always land on his chest. I remember him turning his back to the pass and looking at the blockers across the net. He took his eye completely off the ball, then turned back to it at the last second. He knew exactly where the blockers were going. I couldn't figure out how he did it.

Then there was Ed Skorek, the captain of the Polish team that won the '76 Olympics in Montreal. And Garth Pischke of Canada, Martin Castillo from Mexico, Meche Gonzalez from Peru, and most of the best American players around, like Jon Stanley and Dodge Parker. Of course, I remember Bebeto DeFreitas, the Brazilian setter who came to Santa Barbara to replace Gosciniak, and we were impressed with another Brazilian, Luis Eymard.

Eymard seemed unstoppable. He'd hit these very fast sets, sets that I would later relish on the USA Team, shot out to the left side—slicing angle, more angle, and even more critical angle, until the block moved way inside to stop him. By that time the block was so far inside that he had about five feet of open line. Usually the women played the sidelines on defense and when he finally went for the line, he'd just tattoo one of them. After Eymard drilled the line he would start the whole sharp-angle process over again.

When Eymard, or any hitter, floored—or "six-packed" as it was called—a woman defender with a spike, the hitter was rewarded with a six-pack of beer after the game. Imagine how that promotion would go over in today's world! But some of the women, like Linda Fernandez, would stick in there and hold their own. We thought that was cool.

As good as some of those players were in the IVA, I knew it wouldn't be like watching a real international match—certainly not the Olympics. I had waited so long to see volleyball on TV in the 1976 Olympics that when it finally arrived I had to stay glued to the screen day after day since we had no VCR to tape the broadcast and fast-forward through it. Waiting, waiting, waiting. They showed only about thirty minutes.

After all the pictures I had studied of these Olympians, I only got to see a little of the Soviet-Poland finals. The biggest reason more volleyball wasn't televised was simple—there was no USA Team playing. We hadn't qualified for the 1972 or 1976 Olympics, having been beaten by Cuba both times. We always had good athletes playing volleyball in this country, but the national team program was amateur—part-time at best—and it was impossible to compete against the Soviet bloc countries, Japan, and Cuba, whose teams were effectively full-time professionals.

My three years at Santa Barbara High School (it had no ninth grade) were a wonderful experience—certainly in volleyball, which was a major focus.

We had a great coach, Rick Olmstead, who was a strong influence on me. He worked our tails off and showed us that the more effort you expend the better the results will be. There had been good high school teams in Santa Barbara but they had always been dominated by the powerhouses of the big L.A. schools: Santa Monica High, Palisades, Mira Costa, Newport Harbor, Corona Del Mar, Laguna Beach, San Clemente. Those were the teams that had great volleyball legacies. My first year we finished second in southern California. That was a phenomenal accomplishment, to even get to the finals, though we got crushed by San Clemente. We took third in my junior year and finally won the section championship in my senior year (there was no state tournament then).

My introduction to Olmstead's work ethic in the fall of 1975 was a conditioning program. California interscholastic rules wouldn't allow practice with the coach until January, so during the autumn he gave us a program to "run stadiums." Our high school football stadium had about ten cement rows for seating. We had to scale the big seating rows—by various jumping techniques—then run down the smaller stairsteps. Up and down, up and down, usually a hundred trips. So that meant a thousand jumps: twenty sets of two-legged hops, twenty sets on the right leg, twenty on the left, twenty sprinting, and so on. We did that about four times a week, and it was amazing how many guys stuck with it even though it was voluntary.

If we were playing weaker opponents, Rick would work us for two hours before the match. For example, there was a McDonald's about a mile from the school and he'd have us run there and back. Since that was the same street the visiting teams would use to get to our gym, he made us run the back streets so they wouldn't see us. Rick was such a nice guy that he didn't want to humiliate the visiting team by showing them how hard we worked, even right before crushing them. It was a great feeling. Our high school team had never been that strong and now we were beating most of the best teams in California.

Volleyball was my biggest interest as a teenager. I imagine I was seen by most of my peers as a volleyball jock who got good grades. Most of my friends were guys on the volleyball team. At one point I developed an interest in photography and did quite a lot of shooting, but even then I found myself often down at East Beach shooting my buddies playing volleyball.

Certainly I wasn't one of the coolest guys in school. Clothes weren't an issue for me and never have been. For me, the less clothes on, the better. That must come from all the time I spent on the beach, because in my senior year I decided that I would wear shorts every day of the school year. One winter day it rained so hard that I wore jeans to school, but I quickly changed into my Ocean Pacific shorts at lunch to keep my record perfect. To this day, my preferred attire is shorts and a T-shirt.

Like most kids, I spent time in front of the TV. *Colombo* was my favorite show. His character fascinated me, as did the intricate homicide plots he had to solve. It was that type of story that later appealed to my reading tastes. Traveling so much with the national team, I had a lot of dead time and I used much of it to read mysteries and spy novels—John Le Carre, Sue Grafton, and Agatha Christie were high on my list.

School work came pretty easily to me. I ended up third in my class with a 3.96 GPA and I didn't have to study that hard. I was more into volleyball and hanging out with my friends. Sometimes I'd let some of my pals copy my answers. I had one of those calculators that stores numbers, and I'd help them with a couple of answers on chemistry tests, for example. I wouldn't do that now. I was helping friends cheat, and though I never cheated, it was still wrong.

I did something even worse in my junior year and I learned a very big lesson from it. It resulted in my first brush with the law—one of two in my life—and I've never forgotten it.

Most of us seem to go through a rebellious phase and maybe this was mine. It began as an innocent teenage prank. I had a friend who was rather wild and liked to challenge authority. Walking home from school one day, we happened to find a discarded combination lock from the phys ed locker room and decided what a cool idea it would be to make a key. On the back of those locks was a slot for a master key that would open it and any other lock in the locker room. Our idea was to open some of our buddies' lockers and switch clothes around—dumb pranks like that.

We took the lock apart, figured out how it worked, then got a blank key and filed it down to fit. Meanwhile, my rebellious friend found himself without a clean jersey for phys ed one day, so he decided to open some other guy's locker and borrow his shirt. For some stupid reason we thought it would be funny if he took a few bucks from the guy's wallet too. The victim figured out who it was and turned us in to the principal.

The school authorities wanted to scare us, so they had a couple of plainclothes policemen come on campus and escort us away in front of all the other kids at lunch. Talk about humiliating. We had to go to juvenile court in Santa Barbara, and my friend had to do one hundred hours of school service; I had to do less. We had to pick up trash and help the school custodians after school and at the beginning of summer. The offense wasn't serious by some people's standards, but the fact that I had been an accomplice to theft woke me up. I didn't hang out with my wild friend after that—one instance of shame was enough to straighten me out.

Of course, my parents were very disappointed and angry about the ordeal. One of the best things about playing on the team was riding to matches on the team bus, partly because the cheerleaders rode on it too. Part of my punishment was that I couldn't ride the bus to the games anymore, including the state semifinals at Laguna Beach a few weeks later. Instead, I rode down to Laguna Beach in my dad's car, following the team bus.

A small consolation was that my dad let me drive the car home—a big thing for a sixteen-year-old. We lost the match to Laguna, 3–1. Played like stiffs and finished lower than the year before. After the loss to Laguna, my dad and I got into the car and headed back to Santa Barbara with me driving. I sat a little taller in the seat than he did, and somehow the rearview mirror was blocking my vision of a pedestrian crossing the street at an intersection in Laguna. I just didn't see the person and started going. All of a sudden, my dad screamed at me, "What are you doing?"

Then he made me get out to let him drive. It's a very vivid memory. I felt like I'd screwed up again. That was the topper—a miserable end to a miserable month. The only good thing I remember about the third-place consolation match we played against Mission Viejo High School was that

Al Scates saw me play for the first time. I had written him a letter earlier that year telling him I was impressed with UCLA, the program, and his coaching.

As a teenager, volleyball had provided me with many wonderful experiences and taken me to a lot of interesting places. I'd also been introduced into the cast of colorful characters that makes up the sport, particularly the beach game. But all of this had been confined to Southern California. I was soon to get my first taste of a far bigger game, in a far bigger arena, and things for me would never be the same.

CHAPTER FOUR

EARLY TASTES

Our sport has been around a little over one hundred years. For most of that time in this country, people played it for fun but not as serious competition. That happened in Asia and Eastern Europe. How strange that a small group of American guys—who came of age in Southern California in the late 1970s—would go on to dominate the volleyball world. I was one of them and I got a glimpse of that bright future in the summer of 1977.

At sixteen I knew I'd be one of the youngest players trying out for the Junior National Team because the age limit was twenty and under. That meant I'd be competing against college players. There was some great talent out there—guys who would be future stars of the USA Team—like Dusty Dvorak, Tim Hovland, Steve Salmons, and future beach star Sinjin Smith. There were so many good players that other future stars, like Pat Powers and Craig Buck, were cut from the team.

I made the first cut but I was following a brutal schedule. I got a summer job helping redo the foundation of a friend's house in Santa Barbara. We worked from seven in the morning until two in the afternoon. Then I'd jump in my car and drive the hundred miles to Loyola Marymount University in L.A. for the late afternoon Junior National Team workouts. After three or four hours of practice, I'd drive back home.

I soon learned that guys who were known college stars enjoyed a far different status than a high school kid. That first became obvious when we had to run a mile for time at least once a week. The great players strolled through it in eight minutes or so—they knew they wouldn't get cut for a slow time in the mile, no matter what the coaches said.

But those of us on the bubble were aware that we had better kill ourselves in the mile, and everything else, to even get a shot at making the team. My fastest mile was around a 5:50, and I recall we were lapping guys like Hovland. They were just chuckling at us, "Don't run so hard, guys! You're gonna get cut anyway."

It didn't deter me. Working hard in practice was something I already knew well from playing for Olmstead for two seasons in high school. He showed us how hard work could improve us dramatically. I decided early on that if I was going to be at a practice and the coach said to do twenty-five reps, I'd do at least twenty-six reps. Sure, there were times I thought a drill was pointless, but why expend energy resisting a coach's decision? Just do it seemed the best answer.

Working hard individually is what builds a team collectively. Indoor volleyball is a team sport and there is a simple activity that has always shown a player's commitment to a team. It's called "shagging." A good example occurs in defensive drills where a coach, standing on a table, pounds balls at three players on the court. The drill requires at least a hundred balls to complete, so the players who are out of the drill have to keep gathering the balls and getting them back to the coach quickly—shagging. A surrounding player can meander around, picking up balls casually and using that time to rest, or he can run and shag balls seriously. I prided myself on shagging really well. No one ever saw me shirking that responsibility. I ran after balls, picked up as many as I could, and got them back to the drill. Maybe it's a result of one of my idiosyncrasies—a need for order—because a basket full of balls and none on the floor was a cleanup job done right. It was pleasing to my eyes. If I can borrow a principle from thermodynamics, balls lying all over the gym seemed like entropy at work and it bothered me.

But it went beyond that for me in shagging balls. Safety was part of it—protecting your teammates—and in a team sport that was very important. I had to purposefully remind myself of those things during practice because they usually don't come naturally and they diminish with fatigue. Get tired, get careless. Another great example of the idea of team play is in what we call hitter coverage. If you watch films of my years on the USA Men's Team, you'll see that I never stood and watched the ball after it was set. I always ran in and tried to get as close as I could to the spiker, getting down and ready to pick up the ball in case he was blocked. Saving a ball that looks like a sure point for the other team can turn a game around. It's all about helping your teammates.

After running the mile for time during the Junior National tryouts, we'd go into the gym and do the "Korean circuit"—a series of different kinds of jumps and sprints. Then came a series of "360s," which meant sprinting to a floor line, touching it, then returning to touch the previous line. There might be thirty lines to sprint to in all, and it was excruciating. It had to be done in a certain time period. You were assigned to a group of guys, and if each player didn't make the required time, the whole group had to run the drill again. Here were these name players in our group, who commanded so much respect, and there was no way I wanted to answer to one of those guys by making them run again.

After the initial cuts down to fifteen or sixteen guys, they took us up to Squaw Valley, California, for some high-intensity, high-altitude training. That was the most brutal thing I'd ever been through—three workouts per day. The only thing comparable was my workouts with Olmstead, but I still wasn't prepared for being so sore that I could barely walk after the first few days. The last cut came down to Scott Steele or me. He was a better setter than I was, but I was younger by almost four years and taller, and I assume I made it because of my long-term potential. Dusty Dvorak was the first setter and I was the second. So I was the last guy to make the team—and the youngest.

We flew to Honolulu for the Pacific Rim Tournament, which was my first international competition. I remember walking into the gym and seeing two matches going on at the same time. China was playing on one court and my eyes happened to rest on a Chinese player running a play I'd never seen before. He had legs the size of a horse—in fact, we called him "Horse Legs"—and he hit a kind of hanging set where he broad-jumped about ten feet away from the setter, landing right next to him. The blocker couldn't follow him because he was flying through the air. Then he hit the ball so hard that it almost bounced over the forty-foot-high net separating the two courts. My mouth fell open.

It was an awesome experience and we lost only two matches—to China and to Mexico, each a really close five-gamer. It opened up a whole new world to me, even though I only played about three minutes the entire tournament. To see such great athletes, from different countries I'd only read about, boggled my mind.

My main job was statistician. Pete Fields, the assistant coach, had an elaborate statistical system, and another benchwarmer and I had the assignment of observing and charting each match. Not only was it hard to track all the stats, but it would take an hour and a half later that night with our calculators to figure out the various percentages. Even while taking stats on the other players, I was awestruck by them and learned a lot just by observing.

Soon after the Pac Rims, we flew to Brazil for the 1977 World Junior Championships. We played in several different cities in arenas that held as many as fifteen thousand fans. We won a couple of early-round games and it was looking good for us to finish among the top four teams. In the semi-final round we faced Brazil. I remember that they had installed some auxiliary lighting that hung from the huge ceiling. In the warm-up these Brazilian kids were pounding the ball so hard that they knocked out some of the light bulbs some sixty feet above us. We looked at each other in amazement and muttered, "Oh, my god!" They crushed us in the match too, 3–0.

We bounced back the next night with a strong match against Japan, winning 3–2, so all we had to do was beat Mexico to make the final four. We lost, 3–1, crushing our hopes of becoming the first USA volleyball team of any kind to finish fourth or better in a world competition.

I remember Sinjin Smith wasn't playing much, so he went to the beach every day even though we were ordered not to. He was the rebel of the team. Finally I decided to loosen up a bit and go with him a couple of times since I was hardly playing either. My only role to that point was taking stats.

In Sao Paulo, we played Korea in what was an anticlimactic event, since we were vying for seventh place. The coach, Dick Montgomery, put me in the second game (it was my only chance in the whole tournament to play) and I was really fired up. I had been serving all summer against the first team, so my float serve was particularly strong. I served a bunch of aces, dug a few balls, and ran the offense. Our guys, and probably the Koreans, weren't into the game much but I was in heaven.

We rushed back to Rio that afternoon so we could watch the last two matches of the final four. China crushed Mexico, and then the Soviets—who had pelted us early in the tourney—faced Brazil with fifteen thousand fans going nuts. It was a spectacular match, with first one team and then the other hammering ball after ball. I remember seeing the Soviets do something radical—they passed the whole court with just two players, like a beach pair, just as our USA Team would start doing six years later. And I remembered the faces of many great players whom we would confront in national team competitions, including the Olympics, in the years to come.

That summer of 1977 was critical for guys like Hovland, Salmons, Dvorak, and me—many of whom would become the pillars of the 1984 Olympic team. Four of the six '84 starters played either that summer or the next summer on the Junior National Team. What it mostly gave us was a perspective on what we were up against—how good those other teams were. Here were kids our own age, and in order to catch them by 1984 it was going to require a hell of a lot of work.

Some people make impressions on you that last forever. Mike Normand did that for me. It happened during my only beach tournament of that summer of 1977—right before the final cut of the Junior National Team. I played with Marco Ortega in the Marine Street AA in Manhattan Beach.

Marco and I started well, cruising through the tournament until we met Sinjin Smith and Mike Normand in the quarter-finals. That happened to be Sinjin's first beach tournament ever. Of course, he had played a lot on the beach at Sorrento Beach in Santa Monica but never in tournaments. I knew him because we were both trying out for the Junior National Team at the time. I also knew who Normand was. So did a lot of people. Ex-UCLA star, great jumping ability, volatile personality. His fiery antics had earned him the nickname "Stormin' Normand." There were also some other things in his past that I would soon find out about.

We were playing two-out-of-three games to eleven points. Marco and I jumped out to a lead and were beating them 8–2 or so, thanks to Normand who had given us some free points on unforced errors. I was pretty fired up and looked over at Marco just before he served. I told him, "Keep serving Normand. He's choking."

I didn't think I said it that loud, but Sinjin later told me I did—at least loud enough for Normand to hear me. Next thing I heard was Normand screaming, veins popping out of his neck. "What! Did you hear what that f***ing punk called me? He called me a f***ing choke!" His voice was literally thundering down the beach. Everybody could hear him.

My dad was there watching, stunned like everyone else. And there I was, shaking with fear. I'd never even been in a fight growing up, so I didn't know how to defend myself. Normand's tirade went on, louder and louder, until he finally finished with this: "I'll tell you what. If you beat us, I'll suck your d***. But if we beat you, I'm gonna beat the s*** out of you!" At that point, I was ready to cry. I was only sixteen. Thank God, I had no idea at the time that he had been a Green Beret in Vietnam and was a martial-arts specialist who could have killed me with his bare hands, or I probably would have soiled my pants right there.

Finally, Marco decided to call a time-out so I could try to get back my composure. But I had completely lost it. He had me so scared that I don't think we got another point that game. We lost the next one something like 11–4. They went on to win the tournament and Sinjin got his AAA rating in his very first tournament. If I hadn't opened my stupid mouth, we might have beaten them and gone on to win the tournament. And I might have earned my AAA at sixteen. Then again, I could have been dead.

Normand never said a word to me after the game. I was expecting him to beat my face in. In fact, that's what I kept thinking through the whole match: "I'm gonna get beat up. I'm gonna get beat up." But he just walked off. That is the most intimidated I've ever been on the court. Of all the hostile crowds we've played in front of—twenty thousand people spitting at us, fans throwing batteries at us in places like Brazil and Puerto Rico—nothing ever phased me after that experience. In retrospect, I have to thank Mike for putting me through that because from that time on I became mentally tough. But I sure lost it that day. Still shaken after the Normand episode, we lost our next match to knock us out of the tourney and I practically ran off the beach.

Right after that tournament I left for my first international competition. Only sixteen, but after that experience with Stormin' Normand, I was ready for the world.

I came back to start my high school senior year, older and wiser, after my trip to Brazil and that memorable encounter with Normand. All my buddies on the volleyball team were excited to hear about my trip, and we were frothing at the mouth to start the season since we had come so close to winning the Section championship the previous two years. This would be our last chance.

As a high school team the rules wouldn't allow us to practice in the fall so we formed our own USVBA club team and drove two hours to Los Angeles for tournaments. We got a local restaurant to sponsor us and print up T-shirts with names on them. I was Captain K.

When the season finally rolled around we were ready. We went undefeated and lost only three games—not matches—all year. The second game we lost is very vivid in my memory. It came in a big high school tournament in Santa Barbara. We were playing a weak team in pool play so Olmstead subbed in our second team during the first game. We went on to barely lose the game, but it was meaningless since he put the starters back in and we easily won the match. Still, Olmstead called us into the locker room afterward. Everyone was wondering what could have been on his mind when he suddenly flung his ring of keys against the blackboard and roundly berated us for losing the game.

"There's no excuse for losing a game to that team! If you let yourselves get beat by a team of that caliber, even a game, then what's gonna happen against a good team?" he bellowed. It served to wake us up and enabled us to refocus for the rest of the season. After two years of getting close, we beat Laguna Beach 3–0 for the Section title.

Off the court, I started my senior year with a tarnished reputation because of the locker incident the year before. That bothered me, but I realized it was a mistake and I decided to turn it around. I almost fell over when my senior class voted me Most Outstanding Boy at the end of the school year. I hadn't expected to be able to win back my classmates' trust and respect to that degree. With the team title, as well as having been chosen Section Player of the Year, I ended my high school experience feeling that I had redeemed myself on a couple of levels.

All the guys on the team had spent so much time together and grown so close that I was really disappointed when we graduated—I didn't think I'd ever be on a closer-knit team. Now we were going our separate ways, to different colleges.

After graduation, it was back to the beach. I entered the Hermosa Beach Open, the third or fourth Open I'd ever played, with Marco Ortega. Of all people to draw in the second round, we came up against Mike Normand and his partner! We lost and, of course, there wasn't a peep heard from me. But Marco and I started buzzing our way through the losers' bracket, knocking off team after team—including beating Normand—to be guaranteed at least fourth place and our AAA rating. Sweet revenge. On Sunday afternoon we found ourselves playing in the finals against Menges and Lee, who were the best team on the beach. I remember that I was trying too hard. Instead of relaxing and just playing, I got too tight and made a lot of unforced errors. We lost pretty badly.

Still, I was only seventeen and now had my AAA rating—the highest you could get. I was ecstatic. Afterward, I entered a bar for the first time, the famous Poop Deck (it's still there across the boardwalk), and even had a sip of beer. When I got home that night I was so excited that I went over to John Hanley's and threw pebbles up against his window to wake him up. I just had to tell someone about finishing second in an Open.

Earlier that same summer I had asked Sinjin to play in a tournament and he said no. He wanted to keep playing with his brother, Andrew. Now, with the biggest tournament of the summer coming up—the Cuervo World Championships at Redondo Beach—I was agonizing between Marco and Don Shaw, who had also asked me to play. Don was older, bigger, and stronger, so I went with him. We were rolling until we met Gary Hooper and Steve O'Bradovich in the finals of the winners' bracket on Sunday. We got off to a good lead, then Don started cramping even though it was only our second match that morning. Cramping on the beach virtually translates to losing. I tried to cover for him, but to no avail.

Cramping has always been a part of beach volleyball lore, especially before the pro era. In earlier times, the winners' bracket consisted of two-out-of-three games to eleven points—today it's one game to fifteen. Playing hard for several hours in ninety degree heat burns a lot of your body's energy. It's essential to keep it replenished in order to stave off muscle cramps.

The first time I ever won the Manhattan Beach Open—considered the Wimbledon of beach volleyball—I saw firsthand what cramping does. It was 1980 and Sinjin Smith and I were facing Jim Menges and Matt Gage in the finals. They had to fight through the losers' bracket, and Menges made the mistake of going into the cool ocean after earning a berth in the finals. He got into waist-high water and his legs locked up with cramps. He told me he almost drowned. Luckily, some woman he didn't know dragged him out of the water to safety.

Somehow he got loose enough to walk around, but as he was stepping over a beach chair to enter the court for the finals, his legs locked up again. He got them loose enough to start the game, then fell to the sand after we went up 3–0, and told us he couldn't go on. It was a very anticlimactic to win my first Manhattan Open—and that's why I've never gone into the water during a tournament since.

One famous cramping story occurred in the Manhattan Beach Open in the '60s. It centered around all-time great player Gene Selznick, who was just as famous for his antics off the court. Selznick was a consummate showman. He was also known for his dancing skills, and won several major dance contests in L.A. in the '60s and '70s.

Maybe he'd danced too much the night before, because he started cramping during the finals. Those were the days when drinking was allowed on the beach and Sunday afternoon turned into a giant, wild beach party. Selznick didn't drink, but many of the fans did and they loved his showmanship. So, when his thighs started to cramp in the finals, some of his admirers threw trash onto the court after every play in order to buy time so they could run out, lift the stiff-legged man to his feet, and walk him around until his muscles loosened up. Enough to get him ready for the next serve. There was no time limit, so typically Selznick used it to his advantage and got the crowd in a frenzy—to the point that his two opponents finally came unglued and lost. The story goes that he was carried off the beach in full glory by his inebriated howling fans. A true Bacchanalian scene.

I've cramped a few times myself. It's a result of the number of matches you have to play and how much time you have between games to take in more fuel and water. If you're playing your way back through the losers' bracket, you have to win about seven games on Sunday to go all the way. That's eight hours of playing with only about twenty minutes rest between games, which doesn't give your stomach enough time to empty. You can't eat as much as you'd like. Your energy stores become so depleted that eventually the legs go, then sometimes the stomach, back, and arms. I've seen guys go into complete body cramps—even the neck and fingers.

When every muscle is contracting violently into a ball, the pain is unimaginable. It's a hideous sight. I saw that happen to Gary Hooper one time at Laguna Beach. Paramedics had to come and carry him off the beach. Usually IVs are given to rehydrate a player, but sometimes a muscle relaxant is also given if it's bad enough.

It would be a long time after high school before I would have my first experience with cramping. When you're seventeen and playing hours every day on the beach, you stay in pretty good shape. In the summer of 1978 I fit in about four beach tournaments while again spending most of my time competing on the Junior National Team. We won the Pac Rim tourney this time. And now I was thinking about an approaching adventure. College.

In that era, only a handful of colleges offered volleyball scholarships. Two schools recruited me out of high school: UCLA and USC. First I met with USC's coach, Ernie Hicks. He was a nice enough guy but didn't strike me as a particularly gifted coach or strong personality. He came up to Santa Barbara, met with my parents and me, and explained USC's program and my potential role in it. Since I had been a setter in high school—delivering the ball to my spiking teammates—I was intending to play that position but USC had Dusty Dvorak. I'd already played with Dusty on the Junior National Team and knew he was probably the best setter in the country. He also had two more years of eligibility. So I got the impression that I would have to wait two years before I could play as a starter—regardless of how good a setter I was. I was no Dusty Dvorak and never would be.

Next we drove down to meet Al Scates in the San Fernando Valley, his suggested rendezvous as being halfway between Santa Barbara and where he lived. We later learned that while we had driven over sixty miles, Al had driven only about two miles from his house. He could have ridden his bike to the Denny's where we met! I still like to remind him that it was the easiest recruiting trip he ever made.

Academically, I thought I could make either school as challenging as I wanted. But Al said all the right things. The NCAA allows each school only five full scholarships to spread amongst twelve players. Essentially I was offered tuition, room, and board. That was as good a deal as can be found in college volleyball.

Finally, there was something special about UCLA. After all, it had the dominant volleyball history of any college in the nation. I decided that's where I'd go.

BEST OF THE BRUINS

My first day of college was also my first day of practice at UCLA. I had three or four classes, then ran down to the gym to get my locker and my "roll," which was a rolled-up towel with shorts, tank top, socks, and jock inside. Denny Cline, the assistant coach, started us right away with the "circle drill"—basically, running in a circle around the perimeter of the gym until he yelled, "Okay, down and thirty push-ups!" Or "down and forty sit-ups!"

That first year I got a lot stronger, and I attribute most of it to the circle drill. We worked up to 300 push-ups during that fifteen-minute exercise. I also put a lot of weight on my six-feet-two-inch frame, going from 172 to 185 pounds—mostly muscle. Living in the dorms, I ate at the dorm cafeteria where I could eat as much as I wanted. And I did.

Men's volleyball starts in September and goes until early May—one of the longest seasons in collegiate sports. You have to be very organized in your life, particularly if you're serious about your studies. My dad had set a great example of organization and preparation, but I also learned it firsthand in a calculus class at UCLA. The professor's name was Ray Redhcffer. He was an amazing guy, known for reciting long poems, performing gymnastic moves in class, and memorizing every one of his students' faces and names—some two hundred of them. He taught by assigning us two solid hours of homework a night but nothing on weekends. As a result, I did so much work during the week that I didn't even have to study for the midterm or the final. I was already totally prepared. It was a lesson I've never forgotten.

At the time, there was no pre-med major at UCLA. Since I was into the sciences in high school I chose biochemistry, which was reputed to be the second-hardest major behind theoretical physics. I figured I'd go on to be a doctor—not from any burning desire, but because I was very familiar with it growing up. Biochem would give me a fundamental basis for learning about why people lose their health and how to help them get it back. I felt that whatever specialty I chose in medicine, curing people would boil down to a molecular level.

That's how my mind works—I like to build from the bottom up. For example, some people like to learn a foreign language from conversational tapes, but I can't learn from a smattering of information here and there. When I learned Italian, I couldn't learn it piecemeal. I needed a complete foundation. I learned verb conjugations, grammar rules, and the other most basic elements of the language. How else would you know, for example, about the simple word "the"? As it turns out, there are many forms of "the" in Italian. I guess you'd say I'm more of a linear, sequential thinker.

In my freshman year I was lucky to have a great roommate, Fred Fehl. He was from the San Diego area and I admired him. I also learned from the sense of balance he strove for in his life. Although he studied hard for his biology major, he worked out and had a social life too—a nice girlfriend back home whom he saw on weekends. I, on the other hand, had no social life and felt like I was a bookworm/volleyball nerd.

Fred was going into medicine as I planned to, and he taught me great study habits. Sometimes we'd study in our room; other times we'd organize study sessions with his friends in unlocked classrooms, using the blackboard if we wanted. I was probably closer to Fred than my teammates—we spent so much time together studying.

I got along well enough with all the volleyball players, especially Peter Ehrman and Dave Saunders, but my classes seemed so hard that I never had time to hang out with them. I didn't party with them at all. That came later on.

Regimented I was. Yet every now and then I'd get an urge to step outside my character—in a harmless way. One such time was during my sophomore year when a bunch of us were eating in the campus cafeteria and one of the guys had left a small amount of Dr. Pepper in his glass. Someone decided to throw a piece of beef in it. Another guy added hot sauce, and that was the cue to see who could add something more disgusting to the concoction—yogurt, soup, anything that was on the table— just to see how gross we could make it. The so-called cherry-on-top came when someone swatted a fly buzzing around the table. It was stunned but alive, so I tossed it in.

I said, "Guys, how much will you give me to drink this?" They looked at each other and decided on something like twenty-five bucks each. So I downed it. It blew them away. Ehrman, who was from Hawaii, was so impressed that he bought me an aloha shirt rather than give me the money. It was the nicest shirt I had for most of my college years.

On weekends I'd often go home to Santa Barbara. A week before leaving for UCLA my freshman year, I'd helped my parents move into a new home they had built, and I wanted to enjoy it too. I'd mostly go home just to get away, to do a little studying, but mostly to relax, lay out by the pool, and escape from my other life at UCLA.

Right away, it seemed to me that the head coach, Al Scates, had me pegged to play a big role on the team. Dave Olbright, one of the two starting setters, had graduated the year before so there was a setter spot open. Sinjin Smith, who was a senior, already had one locked up.

Sinjin became my pepper partner on that very first day of practice. I've spent thousands of hours playing pepper and you soon learn that it's more enjoyable to play with someone you like as a person, as well someone who has the same skill level as you. I don't know who really initiated that we be pepper partners, but I think Al wanted the two setters to be together— to push each other.

Scates had rarely run a 5–1 system to that point, where one setter sets every ball to the other five players (five spikers), even though today it is the norm. He went with the two-setter system—a 6–2, it's called—with Sinjin and me. The biggest difference in the two systems is that both setters in the 6–2 also spike when they are in the front row, which means that all six players play as spikers. In the 5–1 the setter doesn't spike, since his sole responsibility is to set every ball. I wasn't a very good hitter that first year. My hitting percentage was .167, which was just above horrendous. But Al was good at keeping a player's confidence up, and I suspect that he privately told Sinjin not to set me very much, though I never heard about it.

That year marked the first-ever undefeated season for UCLA in NCAA volleyball. We had several exceptional players. Steve Salmons was probably the keystone of that team; he was a phenomenal blocker, one of the best I've ever seen. He was also a great hitter. Sinjin was a great all-around player. Rick Amon was a starting middle blocker with a spectacular jump. We also had Casey Keller who, at six feet seven inches, we thought was a giant. Players are a lot bigger these days. Last year UCLA's starting team averaged that height. I think the Dutch team that won the Olympics in Atlanta averaged six feet ten inches. And we had three other strong outside hitters—Peter Ehrman, Greg Giovanazzi, and Joe Mica. There were too many to play at once, so Al had to struggle to get them all enough playing time.

Anyway, I considered myself very fortunate to be surrounded by such incredible talent. In any team sport you'll gain nothing by resenting or feeling jealousy toward teammates. It's much better to surround yourself with the best possible players, form the best team, and hope to win. That way everyone will be able to share the credit.

It turned out that USC, rather than the defending NCAA champion Pepperdine—returning six starters from the championship team the year before—was the team we had to worry about that year, even though we handled USC relatively easily most of the season, beating them every match. It gave us a false sense of security. 'SC had a great squad, including Pat Powers, Dusty Dvorak, and Tim Hovland, who would all go on to become volleyball legends.

Going into the 1979 NCAA finals in May, I felt pretty good—until a bad omen seemed to appear on the Friday of the semis. I always prided myself on being on time, but I had been up until 4:00 A.M. finishing a couple of chemistry projects the previous two nights. After handing in my projects that Friday, I decided to take a little nap before practice. More than little—I slept through the alarm I had set. Somehow I woke up and sprinted to Pauley Pavilion, arriving fifteen minutes late—late for the first and only time in my UCLA career. Fortunately, we were playing Ohio State and it was a cakewalk.

The next night USC came out on fire for the finals. They were winning the first game 14–12, when Salmons passed a ball behind me and I tried to run it down. I took it with my hands and tried to fling it high to the other side of the court. It was a pretty poor set, ten feet inside and right on the net. Sinjin came screaming in and jumped to hit it. In the process, he came under the net and Dusty Dvorak landed on him, breaking Dusty's leg. Later, and only half-jokingly, Sinjin called that the best play he made all season. It probably was. From the opening serve, Powers had been drilling balls from the ten-foot line. No one had ever done that back then, but after losing Dusty, USC was a different team. Bill Stetson came in and they won the game, but we won the next three. Joe Mica, a starter the year before, came off the bench to play a great match for us, and Sinjin was voted Most Valuable Player.

Al Scates was a great game coach. Being a great player in the '60s, he brought his own playing experiences into his coaching. Cagey, innovative, he excelled at making good player substitutions and finding the weaknesses in opposing teams. Above all, he instilled his own sense of confidence in his players.

I'll always remember an incident during my sophomore year when our UCLA team was invited to play in Japan. We found ourselves getting crushed by their top all-star team. They had won the first two games and were winning the third when Scates sauntered into the huddle, gave us a big smile and a chuckle, and said, "All right, Karch, I want you to run a play and give the set to Salmons for a sideout. Randy [Stoklos], they're then going to set outside, their hitter is going to hit line, and you're going to stuff it. Then they're going to set the same guy and, Salmons, you're going to smother his angle."

It all happened just as he planned, and we proceeded to come back and shock their team 15–2 in the fifth game. Al would say it, we would do it, and we'd win. His teams were seen as cocky, but his players viewed it as giving them confidence and a positive outlook. He had high expectations and he always emphasized the final goal—winning the NCAA championship. Clearly he's been driven by that goal. He just became the winningest coach in college sports history when UCLA beat Pepperdine for its, and his, seventeenth NCAA championship.

Rick Olmstead had taught me in high school how hard I could work and how important preparation is. Except for the push-ups and sit-ups in the circle drill at UCLA, most days I worked less hard in college than I ever did in high school. However, Al taught me about trusting my own abilities, about never thinking you're out of it—having confidence not only in yourself but in your teammates as well. If we mucked up a play, Al would yell, "Forget that play! Think about the next one!"

We found out that it worked.

I'd had good coaches up to then, but I didn't have as much luck with the USA Men's Team in 1979. That summer I had my first tryout with the team in Chicago—for the Pan-American Games. Things for the USA Men's Team were in disarray during that era. In 1975 there was a huge blowup with dissatisfied players, and most of the better ones had jumped to the IVA pro league. At that point Doug Beal became the head coach of the USA Men's Team and led a movement to get a national training center in Dayton, Ohio.

From all accounts, it was disastrous. The intent to stay together year-round was good, but Dayton was not the place to do it. California players would stay for a month, sweat in the humidity or freeze in the cold, then jump in their cars and head back to the coast. In 1979 Beal decided to go back to playing and give up the coaching to another Midwesterner, Jim Coleman. Although Jim was the coach of the 1968 Olympic Team, he didn't enjoy a glowing reputation as a head coach. Nor did Beal, for that matter—at least not among Californians.

In Chicago, Coleman had taken six veterans off the existing national team and automatically put them on the Pan-Am squad—without a tryout. These six guys came from a team that had recently finished seventh place in the NORCECA Championships (the International Volleyball Federation has divided the world into five zones for Olympic qualification purposes, and the U.S. is in the NORCECA, or North, Central American, and Caribbean zone), which was probably the worst finish in American volleyball history. Consequently, those automatic spots on the team seemed questionable to some of us, especially since some were Midwesterners—like Beal and Coleman.

Later I found out that politics had always been a factor in selecting national teams and, unfortunately, probably always will be. In 1964 Gene Selznick, arguably our best player, was cut from our first Olympic team because of his ongoing conflict with the USVBA.

Now the tryouts for the remaining six spots were between the young talent from California, guys like Dvorak, Hovland, Powers, Salmons, and me.

I had a really good tryout. I did well in the drills and physical tests, and I played well in the scrimmages. Another guy who had an even better tryout was Brian Ehlers. I pride myself on court sense—knowing exactly where the ball, and all the players, are on the court at all times—but Brian had the best court sense I've ever seen. Perhaps it was due to his deafness, because he always seemed more aware than the rest of us. We played the year before on the Junior National Team, and during some matches in very loud gyms, when it was impossible to hear on the court, I could just turn and mouth words to him. He could read lips impeccably.

One time, in the 1978 Pacific Rim tournament, we were in the middle of a substitution when a player on the other team served the ball. Somehow, the ref ignored the substitution and blew the whistle, so the serve was legal although neither team was even looking. Except for Brian. He ran all the way across the court to bump the serve back over the net, where it dropped untouched for a sideout. That's the kind of court sense he had.

I liked Brian a lot. My wife, Janna, who also attended Pepperdine, told me about a time she and her friends had gone out with him, before I knew her. She said he was very courteous, but it was difficult to hear in his van because he turned the huge speakers way up so he could feel the music. He was a really good dancer too, all through feeling the vibrations.

On the last day of the tryouts Coleman called Brian into the room to tell him he was cut. I remember him coming out crying and I asked myself, "Did the coaching staff watch the same tryout that we were at?" They never should have cut him. I also thought their mistake might end his career, because he had just graduated from college and he had nowhere else to play in order to keep improving. I believe he could have made the 1984 Olympic team, but now people will never know what a great player he was.

Then I got called into the room. Coleman complimented me on an outstanding tryout, but the problem was me being a student. He wanted me to drop out of UCLA that fall so that I could move to Dayton and train fulltime to prepare for the 1980 Olympic qualification tournament in Bulgaria in January. He felt that every player on the Pan-Am team had to make that commitment. I couldn't sacrifice interrupting my college education for that proposition—especially for a less-than-good chance of even qualifying for the Olympics. I walked out of the room with tears too.

That was the only time I ever got cut from a team, even though I played a part in the decision. Apparently I made the right one. My friends on the team had only horror stories of the Pan-American Games in Puerto Rico. They said the referees stopped letting them wipe up sweat on the court, even though it was ninety degrees with ninety-percent humidity inside the gym, so the footing was treacherous and every time a player ran to jump, he'd just slide right under the net where the blockers might land on him. That's how Salmons's back problems started.

The coaching was worse. There was internal dissension and a lack of leadership. The most common rumor was that the coaches ended the competition by throwing dice to decide the starting lineups.

My consolation came in the summer of 1979 when the USVBA sent another Junior National Team to the Pacific Rims in Hawaii. I played in that, as well as in the following World University Games in Mexico City. I loved all the traveling. At eighteen there is no better way to grow up and establish your independence.

I also had some fun. After Tim Hovland and I finished our stint with the Junior team, we stayed in Hawaii to play in the Hawaii State Beach Open. Hovland is not only one of the greatest players ever—indoor or beach—but is one of the most colorful personalities in the sport. On or off the court. I loved being around him—we seemed to be the yin and yang of volleyball. He was the explosive, spontaneous, charismatic side; I was the controlled, planned, logical side.

The tournament was at the Outrigger Canoe Club in Honolulu, and I remember the people there had never seen Hovland play. Their eyes were bugging out of their heads. Hovland was like a volcano. He was cocky and brash, but he competed so fiercely—and so vocally—that he just grabbed them by the throats and got their attention.

We came through the losers' bracket to win, and there was one play during our march back to the finals that typified Hov so well. He made a great dig and I put the set right on the net. Being the consummate entertainer, he had been trying all tournament to hit the ball so hard that it would bounce over the twenty-foot, wire-mesh fence surrounding the court. To do that you have to hit the ball straight down, close to the net, and here was a set to do it. Trying a little too hard, Hov drilled it right in the net. All of a sudden, his face contorted and he took the net and yanked it as hard as he could, almost pulling it off the posts. The next thing he did I didn't even see, but someone told me later. Waiting for the next serve and still fuming with all this frustration, he suddenly leaped from a standing position and did a backflip! Not bad for a guy six-foot-five.

People were riveted watching him. They either loved him or despised him. It was the same with his coaches. There was no middle ground with the Hov—and it's still that way with him.

There were times when Sinjin Smith and I felt invincible. During our first summer playing together in 1979, we entered five beach Opens and won every one of them. We continued to play through 1984, but my commitment to the USA Team left me less and less time to play on the beach. I played only a few tournaments during those last three years.

That was an era before blocking became such a force in the game. Prior to 1986, a blocker's hands were not allowed to pass over the plane of the net, so defense was limited. That meant finesse—or siding-out—was paramount to winning. Sinjin was that kind of player. In fact, he was the best player at siding-out I've ever seen.

Games were remarkably long in those days, a lot longer than today's pro game, which has a time clock. You really had to work hard to win a tournament. They used a double-elimination format, so you could play as many as six or seven matches a day—with a best-of-three-games-to-eleven-points format in the winners' bracket. Height wasn't such a factor then, since the rules prohibited blocking over the net. Without a blocking threat, the ball was ideally set right on top of the net and hitters would go up and just pound the ball straight down. Defense was limited to digging, so there weren't many rallies, nor any easy points from jump-serving, since that serve hadn't arrived yet. It became a war of attrition—a long, drawn-out affair under a blazing sun. A single game to eleven points could last an hour and a half. As one famous player, Mike Bright, once put it, "It's side out until one guy cramps!" There were a lot of skinny players back then.

Players were svelte for other reasons too. A big one is that many of the top players didn't have much money. Playing beach volleyball was a lifestyle—not unlike surfing—where playing came first and creature comforts second. A lot of guys worked nights as waiters, at restaurants like the Chart House, then played during the day and on weekends. In those days the Chart House was a cool place to work, serving steaks and fish in a relaxed Southern California atmosphere—all the waiters wore aloha shirts.

The tournaments were a lot different then as well. Fans brought their beach chairs and coolers full of beer to the beach, set them down right next to the court, and enjoyed the scene without any restraints. It was a very social, intimate atmosphere that would eventually disappear with professionalism. Things change.

In almost fifty years of organized beach volleyball, aficionados have told me that the finals of the 1979 World Championships in Redondo Beach, California, was one of the best matches ever played. I would agree—for many reasons—but mostly because it illustrated the old, play-until-you-die game at its best.

It was the last regular tournament of the summer and I had spent most of the summer playing indoor volleyball, including competing for the U.S. in the World University Games in Mexico City. I got back on a Wednesday afternoon after literally carrying my packed bags to our last match. Seconds after the final point, I sped to the airport in a taxi to catch an early flight out. Sinjin and I had time for just one good practice on that Thursday, relaxed on Friday, and started play the next day.

After being teammates at UCLA earlier that year, Sinjin and I decided to play together on the beach. I was eighteen and he was twenty-two. We were good buddies. He had a big, close-knit family, with two sisters (a third one had passed away years earlier) and three brothers, and every week they'd all get together for Tuesday Night Dinner. Most of their friends had a standing invitation to those dinners, and they all made me feel so welcome—just like a part of the family. I enjoyed their company as well as Sinjin's aunt's famous lasagna, which was so good that I'd even call ahead to see if she was cooking. I spent the night at their house whenever I didn't have a place, which was often during the summer. I only rented an apartment at UCLA during the school year.

On the court, things clicked too and we won the first two tournaments of the season. What looked like an epic summer on the sand was broken only by my decision to spend most of the summer, after failing to make the Pan-American Team, playing for the Junior National and World University Games teams.

After our hot start, Andy Fishburn and Dane Selznick—son of the legendary Gene Selznick—became the team to beat most of that summer of '79. Somehow they lost in the first round in Redondo but came all the way back through the losers' bracket to face us in the finals on Sunday afternoon. They beat us in a two-out-of-three match that went to the limit,

12–10 in the third game, in an incredible show of stamina. Since we each had one loss, we had to play another game to fifteen—what we call the "double final"—to decide the tournament. I remember that the sun had already set when we started that last game.

The whole crowd stayed to watch in complete darkness. A couple of parking-lot lights were on, but essentially there was no light on the court. Inexplicably, we had better rallies in the darkness than in daylight. I was in for another surprise. The prevailing theory at the time was to serve skyballs when it was dark—sixty or seventy feet up—so the receiving team would lose sight of the ball in the darkness. But what we found was that it gave us more time to get under the ball and line it up, even though it was coming out of a black sky.

It was a battle of wills, with no side showing any weakness. Finally I decided to try a different tactic late in the game—a short, low serve that would barely clear the net. I got four straight aces in front of Selznick, who not only couldn't see the serve but, equally important, he couldn't hear it! That got us up 13–9, but my next serve barely ticked the top of the net. Suddenly they made a quick run to take the lead at 14–13. Then it started going back and forth with sideout after sideout. We edged ahead to 17–16 and I dug a ball that Sinjin ran down and barely got up. All I could do was to take it with my hands and set it over the net, faking a deep shot but placing it short. But Dane guessed right and charged to the net, bumping the ball to Fishburn who then gave him a tight set right on the net. I thought it was an overset so I ran up to play it, but Dane punched the ball over my head—to our back line for a sideout.

I can still see Dane standing there at the net. He was always very tanned, so in the darkness all I could make out were flashes of his bright white teeth. Sometimes he'd give you this big smile after he made a good play—what we used to call his Cheshire grin—and he gave it to me full-force after that play. Almost. The rules at that time stated that your hand couldn't go over the net, whether spiking or blocking. The referee, Butch May, who was a great player in the '60s, softly called out, "Point. You went over the net."

"What!" they both screamed. The judgment was that Dane's finger had broken the plane of the net, which was a violation and gave us the match and the tournament. All four of us were so fatigued that they didn't have the energy to protest the call much further, and we didn't have the energy to celebrate. How Butch ever saw that in the darkness I'll never know, but it was the end of an incredible match. And the end of a valiant effort. No team has ever lost in the first round and come all the way through the losers' bracket to win and they came within a fingernail—literally.

The prize money for that tournament gave us each about $1,000, but NCAA rules stipulated that as a student on athletic scholarship I couldn't receive any money. Since I had given all my prize money to UCLA the year before—and had not even received a thank-you note—I had this money sent to a hospital foundation in Santa Barbara, although technically I don't think the rules even allowed me to stipulate where the money should be donated. I figured the hospital would appreciate it more than the super-endowed university. Not that I didn't appreciate my scholarship to UCLA. On the contrary, I had a great first year there. But they should have sent a thank-you note the first time.

CHAPTER SIX

WESTIES

My sophomore year at UCLA seemed to be jinxed. Scates had organized a tour to Japan and we learned from our hosts that competing in sports there is considered to be a very Spartan exercise. They didn't heat the gyms—even in the winter, which is when we arrived—so it was freezing. It was so cold we could see our breath, the substitutes had to wear two pairs of sweats to stay warm, and during time-outs steam was coming off our players' heads. In keeping with the Spartan theme, the gyms had cement floors and that caused Steve Salmons to reinjure his back after he had hurt it in the Pan-American Games. Salmons was out the rest of the year and had to redshirt—so as not to lose a year of eligibility—which meant we lost our best net player.

We also learned that Japan was crazy for volleyball, with the gyms packed full of thirteen- to twenty-year-old girls screaming for all their favorite Japanese players. Those guys were like rock stars. When the handsomest player would serve, the whole gym seemed to light up from all the camera flashes.

Within a few years our USA Men's Team could boast that we were the best team in the world, and that meant the same idol-worship by fans in Japan and other countries where volleyball was popular. It was crazy at times. We would get letters from around the world—this one was sent to me by a Japanese girl, signed Shizuoka:

When I saw you on television, I couldn't go to sleep in enthusiasm
for hours . . . All of your motion, I love. Do you have a lover or a
wife? If nothing, I want to be your sweetheart.

Returning from Japan meant coming back to reality and more bad
luck. After Sinjin graduated, Randy Stoklos had come to UCLA and
replaced him as the other setter. Then midway through the season, Randy
was coming around behind me to hit a play set—a "fake-X" play it's
called—but he came too close. After I set the ball my left elbow came
down on him as he was jumping up. In another piece of ill fortune, my
elbow broke his nose.

Our luck wouldn't change. The 1980 NCAAs were at Ball State in
Muncie, Indiana, and Randy got really sick before the semis. I'm not sure
it mattered since USC had an incredible team: Dusty Dvorak, Pat Powers,
and Tim Hovland, plus this new junior college transfer, Steve Timmons. In
the regular season, we split the four matches we faced them, but they beat
us 3–1 in the NCAA championship. We were up against one of the greatest teams in college history and it would have been an upset to beat them.
Still, that didn't make losing any easier for us.

Losing in volleyball at UCLA was a pretty rare event. Our record
for the four years I was there was 124–5. After the last point against
USC, I kicked the ball as hard as I could toward the ceiling in the big
arena. The crowd didn't take to that and when they named the all-tournament team, I got a rousing boo. I was really hurt, depressed, and angry.
I went back to my hotel room, and within a few hours I got violently
sick. Diarrhea and throwing up every ten minutes—something you'd
expect in Mexico or Brazil but not in Muncie, Indiana. After three hours
of that, I thought I was going to die. I called my dad, who was staying
in another room, and he got me to the hospital where they gave me a
shot to stop the vomiting.

I was so spent that Randy had to pack for me the next morning. When
I stepped out of the car at the airport, I just slithered to the ground and
laid down in the gutter, my head on the sidewalk. They brought me a

wheelchair to get to the plane. There were two plane changes to make before arriving home—and the end of a long nightmare.

That year I seemed to get the hang of school and studying better so I had more time to socialize and started going to some of the volleyball parties at UCLA. At one of them I met a very striking older girl with a great sense of style who seemed to know all the players. She took me under her wing and I fell for her. Unfortunately, she was Sinjin's girlfriend—he was in Dayton at the time. We went out for a while and at one point I even wrote him to apologize. I knew it was wrong, and that I should have stopped seeing her much sooner than I did. It's something I'm not proud of, but it happened.

Growing up includes making mistakes. It also includes learning about yourself. I tended to have a kind of an antiauthoritarian streak in me back then. I don't know if I got it from my dad—because he resisted the Communist regime—but I had it. One night it surfaced when I was at a party in Santa Monica with all the UCLA volleyball players. It was a big one and when the music got too loud, the neighbors called the police. They showed up, pushed us out of the house, and said we had to leave.

But I had put my backpack with my keys down inside, which proved to be a mistake. It wasn't much of an attempt, but I tried the semi-polite approach and explained to the cop that I couldn't leave because my car keys were inside. He wouldn't listen, so I got irritated and it devolved into an argument. Today, I realize that the police must get tired of dealing with belligerent people at parties, but finally he told me he'd throw me in jail if I didn't leave.

Well, I didn't want to walk fifteen miles home or go home with a friend, but I probably should have. Instead, I walked around to the back of the house and tried to sneak back in. The officer caught me. I was taken to the Santa Monica jail and was given a choice: get booked and leave, or stay overnight in the drunk tank. I chose the overnight stay because I didn't want anything on my record. An unpleasant evening—but poignant.

Other than the locker incident in high school, I'd never had a problem with the police. So this shook me up. That's where I learned I had to squelch that streak in me. There are some defining moments through which you learn when it's appropriate to challenge authority and when it's not. Today, when the game of volleyball has such visibility, I've become very aware of where I go and what I do. It's simple—I don't let myself go near places where there could be trouble like that.

I think much more now about morality and questions of ethics. I've come to believe that your actions—not your intentions, your motives, or what you say you believe—determine what kind of a person you are: decent or indecent, kind or mean-spirited. And those actions add up over time like a balance sheet, so I try to pile up as much on the positive side as I can and keep my bad behavior to a minimum.

I enjoy contemplating ethical issues while listening to the radio. One of my favorite times is listening to author/theologian/talk-show host Dennis Prager, who discusses current moral and ethical topics. He argues that during the last thirty or forty years our social fabric has eroded significantly due to "moral relativism" in this country, as he calls it. He contends that many Americans no longer believe in absolute rights and wrongs—especially as argued by people in higher education and in the media—and that has led to our moral decay. I agree to a large extent with that.

While I'm uncertain about many theological issues, I do believe there are absolute rights and wrongs. It is wrong to murder, to hurt another human being, to take something that isn't yours. Prager feels that it's become politically incorrect to make any judgments about anything. We share the same viewpoint, that you do have to take certain stances as to what is good behavior or bad behavior.

After the NCAAs in 1980, I played in the USVBA National Championships. The team was sponsored by Chuck's Steak House and I played with Chris Marlowe, Denny Cline, and some other former UCLA players. During the tournament I was blocking and the ball hit me on the end of my left little finger, breaking it, although I thought it was only a dislocation. I had Cline pull my finger back in the joint but it popped right back out again, so I taped it and played. A few days later I had it X-rayed. The doctor had to put a screw in it, and I couldn't play for four or five weeks. When Sinjin and I finally played in our first beach tournament, we took a fifth. We'd never lost a tournament and it was a miserable way to start our season.

That would be essentially my one full summer of beach volleyball until 1990. For the next ten years I was mostly devoted to playing indoor for the USA Men's Team. In that 1980 season, Sinjin and I recovered to win six of the last eight tournaments, but I wasn't satisfied with the season—particularly the World Championships in Redondo Beach. I remember a match against Mike Dodd where he was blocking and his partner, Jon Stevenson, was running around picking up every ball on defense. Sinjin wasn't feeling very effective against their schemes, so we switched sides in the middle of the match just to try something new—the only time I've ever done that in a tournament. We just weren't in sync. We took fifth again, and commiserated by drinking some beers and being the last two guys off the beach.

The year following our bitter loss to USC in the 1980 NCAAs, we were able to get some sweet revenge. Steve Salmons, such a key player for us, was again out most of the year, but he came back right at the end of the season and we played a few matches together. Not surprisingly, the NCAA championship once again came down to the last two points—against USC. We were winning 14–13 in the fifth game and served for match point. The USC setter went to John Hedlund and we blocked him. Hovland covered the stuff but the ref, Wink Davenport, called a double hit since the ball touched Hovland twice—a violation. Point, game, match. Needless to say, the Hov almost ripped Davenport off the stand. For us, it was particularly satisfying to see Salmons come back after suffering so much for two years. He gave a phenomenal performance that night, and it was a fitting and deserved ending for his great career at UCLA.

A few weeks after the 1981 NCAA championship, the USVBA moved the USA Team training center to San Diego and tryouts were held. It had been announced that the Olympics would be in Los Angeles, so instantly there was a lot more interest in making the team—we would automatically qualify as the host country—and players wouldn't have to live in Dayton! It was a pretty intense weekend or two. Dvorak, Timmons, Powers, Buck, Sinjin, Stoklos, Dodd, Hovland—an incredible crop of young players—were vying with some of the veterans already on the team such as Paul Sunderland, Marc Waldie, Rich Duwelius, and Aldis Berzins. I made the team.

After spring finals, I threw some stuff in the car and drove down to San Diego for the summer. The USA Team staff promised us some money for living expenses but most of us never saw any of it. We just found a place to crash on someone's floor. Typically, we would practice from 8:00 A.M. to 12:30 P.M, grab a sandwich, drive down to South Mission Beach, then dive in the ocean to wash off our gear. We'd lay it out to dry on the sea wall and play games all afternoon. Sinjin, Hovland, and Dodd were all there, so we had some intense games between what were then considered the top two teams in beach volleyball. Our lifestyle was a pretty mindless, shallow existence with no monetary rewards, but we loved it. We played indoor volleyball all morning, beach volleyball all afternoon, found a floor to sleep on that night, and did it all over again the next day.

In July we went to Mexico City for the NORCECA tournament. This would be the first real test in international competition for us younger guys. Until then, most of us had played against each other in college or in international junior competitions. But this wasn't juniors.

In the finals we faced Cuba, which was among the top four teams in the world, in front of a very hostile crowd. Coach Doug Beal had us in a weird system where I was a setter in two rotations and Dusty Dvorak set in four. Neither of us liked it. Dusty was clearly our best setter and it didn't make sense that I set in two positions, which also took me out of the serve reception. The system hurt us. Still, we played them to 13–13 in the fifth game and had a chance for the fourteenth point when Dusty set Mike Blanchard instead of Hovland on a play set. Mike got roofed and the Cubans scored two straight points. Close but no cigar—certainly not a Cuban one.

The Cubans had historically been our rivals in volleyball and we soon saw that we would continue that tradition. Surely politics had a big role in it, but when we played each other there was an added element of fire.

Those guys were spectacular athletes. No one in the world could jump and hit like they could.

The highest jumpers I ever saw were a couple of Cubans, but that wasn't when I was competing against them. I was in high school, in the '70s, when I saw Diego Lopera and Lionel Marshall. It blew me away. They were only about six feet tall, but rumors were they jumped fifty inches— over four feet off the ground. That's up there. Alexander Savin from the Soviet Union was a great leaper too. He was also six foot seven, which helped to make him one of the greatest spikers and blockers to ever play the game. Playing against him, I remember how tough it was to hit by his incredible block.

Jumping always came naturally to me. I remember that in high school I could take a volleyball, stand on one leg under the basket, jump up, and dunk it. It's a wonderful feeling to hang in midair and look over the net, down at the opposing ten-foot line—like defying gravity, almost gliding through the air.

Since jumping is so critical to volleyball, we were often tested on the USA Men's Team. My best was forty-one inches, but that was after a typical four-and-a-half-hour grueling workout, and then some brutal jump training. If I had been fresh, it could have been higher.

In the end, we could never jump higher than the Cubans, but we would usually beat them. As with the Soviets, we would have some great battles. That first one in Mexico City was a tough one. Still, we were happy, all in all. We were on the right track.

That summer of 1982 the "King of the Beach" title was organized by Event Concepts, a sports promotion company. The winner was to be decided by a cumulative point system of tournament finishes, so Sinjin and I tried to play every tournament we could. I remember that a friend of assistant coach Bill Neville was in San Diego helping out the USA Team as a guest coach. They were always testing us: treadmill, conditioning, strength, blood tests. We felt like guinea pigs and this guest coach, Mike Fleming, helped with the tests. We told him that we were trying to win that "King of the Beach" title, forgetting that he'd probably report straight to Beal. That meant we had to play in the Mission Beach Open in San Diego, even though a USA Team practice was scheduled for Saturday morning and we were leaving for Japan on the following Monday. Sinjin and I convinced the tournament director to enter us in the tournament, charge us with a forfeit in our first match on Saturday morning, and then allow us to arrive in the early afternoon to play through the losers' bracket.

At Saturday's practice Sinjin and I were already antsy, but when Beal announced that a team photo was to be taken, we were dying. It meant we'd have to stay an extra twenty minutes and might miss our second match—forfeiting out of the tournament completely. After the photo, we raced to the tournament and sprinted onto the court. Although the tournament didn't have many top teams entered, we met a pretty good team in that first match. In fact, it turned out to be our toughest match of the whole tournament and we went on to win, going through the losers' bracket.

After arriving in Tokyo, Beal called a meeting with Sinjin and me. Beal had found out, of course, that we played in the beach tournament and he was furious with us for participating without his permission. But we knew that if we had asked, he would have refused anyway. He explained that the beach game was very different from indoors, comparing it to the difference between racquetball and tennis. I countered that it was more like the disparity between hard-court and clay-court tennis. Neither one of us convinced the other.

We beach players thought Doug Beal really didn't know much about the beach game. He had grown up in Ohio. He had no tan. And we certainly never saw him down at Mission Beach. So how could he know much? In Japan, he also told us how he abhorred the adulation we received on the beach, adding that it was too satisfying to a player's ego to play in that environment. Whether that was true or not, we weren't really sure how it pertained to indoor volleyball. In his defense, it had to be admitted that all of us California guys had a mean, antiauthoritarian attitude in us—especially if the figure of authority was a non-Californian.

That attitude surfaced as soon as we arrived at the Tokyo airport, dead tired. There were TV camera crews on hand, which was something new to us. When they started filming us we put on our Ray-Bans in jest, which really upset Beal.

Beal was often angry with us Californians. By that time we had named ourselves the "Westies," and the rift between ourselves and the head coach was already wide. The gap was even wider when it came to Sinjin. He was often chastised for doing something wrong, so we took to mimicking Beal, like, "Hey, Smith, get that toothpick out of your mouth!" Or "Tuck your shirt in, take those shades off, hide that Walkman, and give me twenty!" Beal kept the incessant nagging going, and we egged it on with our sarcasm.

We got along much better with the assistant coach, Bill Neville, because he was a real players' coach—a buffer between us and Beal. We saw Doug as a cold, quiet, standoffish coach who kept his distance and never let us get to know him. I think he chose to act that way. Maybe he and Neville planned the good cop/bad cop routine from the start. In any event, there were a lot of things we didn't like in the player-coach relationship with Beal but we also knew that he was calling the shots, and in the end each player had to make a choice. Am I willing to make the sacrifices to play in the Olympics, to become one of the best teams in the world? And, for the accomplished beach players, can I resist the temptation of a much more enjoyable lifestyle on the sand—just jump in the car with the gang, play in the tournament, party a little, drive back, play all week until another weekend tournament? For a young guy, that was fun. The indoor thing was a real grind.

On that Japanese trip, Timmons and the four beach guys, Hov, Dodd, Sinjin, and I, decided one night to have a little party in our hotel room in Tokyo. They have beer vending machines on the street in Japan and certain machines sell mini-kegs that hold two or three liters. We got a couple, started drinking, and began playing loud music. We were really into music, which was another thing Doug Beal seemed to hate. In those days I was really into groups like the B52s, INXS, U2, and Simple Minds. Timmons brought some little speakers that hooked up to a Walkman and we cranked up the sound, until we heard a knock on the door. Someone ran to the door and looked through the peephole, and through this fisheye lens saw Doug. He still had a Fu Manchu mustache in those days and wore thick glasses, so he looked like some kind of giant insect standing there. In the meantime, Hovland was tossing the plastic kegs out the window whispering, "Get rid of the evidence!"

The next morning we were eating breakfast in the second-floor restaurant and when we looked outside the window, what did we see lying on the roof? Those empty kegs!

We had not learned any discipline yet, which meant we played hard in the day, but stayed up too late and drank too much beer at night. It cost us on the court. We played five matches against the Japanese while we were there and lost all five—four of them by two points in the fifth game. One time we had a 14–4 lead in the fifth and lost. That was the worst comeback we ever allowed. We had only been together a few months, we weren't used to Beal, and we partied too much. Consequently, we couldn't get over the hump in Japan.

Both teams flew back to the States for a tour, and we played the first match in San Diego. It was in front of our friends and that made a difference. We won three out of the four matches in the U.S.

Sinjin and I went back to play in more beach tournaments. By that time the buzz on the beach was about the dream team, Fishburn and Stoklos, who had paired up. But the match proved to be better on paper than on the court. We won six out of seven tournaments that year, including the big one in Redondo Beach. For the next three summers, my playing on the beach would be limited to just one tournament. That was a big sacrifice for me. Sinjin, Hovland, and Dodd were faced with the same decision and they weren't willing to give up the beach—or at least conform to Beal's demands. Admittedly, the beach game was more fun in a lot of ways. For one thing, there's no hard-nosed coach telling you what to do. But I decided that I wanted to play in the Olympics, and so I would grudgingly accept Beal's rules.

By 1982 the old California beach mentality, which had battled with the Midwestern USVBA establishment for so many decades, had firmly invaded the USA Team. The beach guys were pitted against the coaching staff, but the coaches had the final authority. Soon a line in the sand would be drawn for the beach players. I was the only one among them to cross over. I was going to Los Angeles no matter what. Consequently, my days on the sand were essentially over until after the Los Angeles Olympics.

SHOES OR NO SHOES?

It's not every day that you would ask the athletic director of UCLA for a shot of vodka but that's just what I did in January of 1983. It was my first public speaking engagement and I was sweating bullets. The occasion was the annual NCAA convention and an honorary luncheon for 1982's Top Five NCAA Scholar-Athletes. I was selected as one and was asked to accept on behalf of all five winners, another of whom was John Elway.

The banquet was held at a large convention center in the Mission Valley area of San Diego, but I had been given the impression that it would be attended by only about fifty to a hundred people. When we walked onto the dais, I was suddenly staring out at two hundred banquet tables and about two thousand faces! That's when I half-joked to Bob Fischer, our athletic director who was sitting next to me, for a shot of something to calm my nerves. He didn't have any but he gave me as much moral support as he could.

My speech turned out okay, once I got going. I talked about the importance of balance in college sports—how we need to challenge our minds and our bodies every day. I felt, and still feel, that we have to stress academics among college athletes, especially since such an infinitesimal percentage of college scholar-athletes actually make a living afterward as professional athletes. Interestingly enough, at that time the NCAA was looking at making entrance requirements for athletes stricter, as well as requiring a higher grade-point average to maintain eligibility. So my speech was relevant, and it even earned some mention in the *San Diego Union-Tribune* the following day.

It was at the time of that speech that I started going out with my future wife, Janna Miller. I had actually met Janna in the fall of 1982 when I was rooming with a UCLA teammate, Mark Anderson. Mark was from San Clemente, a beautiful beach town about sixty miles south of Los Angeles. His girlfriend, who was going to Pepperdine University at the time, was from San Clemente too. Her name was Janna.

When we first met, what struck me about her was how kind she seemed. To any guy she would have appeared beautiful, but since she was my roommate's girlfriend that aspect didn't capture me. I'd already learned that lesson. She was blonde, athletic, and she looked great in a bikini, but there were lots of shapely girls on the beach. The one physical feature that did capture me—as it did everyone—was Janna's crystal-blue eyes. Even today, I still find myself being mesmerized by them.

Within months, they broke up and I asked her out soon afterward. I knew Janna was a great match for me. She was smart, beautiful, caring, and intuitive. But whether I was or would become right for her, I was less sure about. I was only twenty-two, as was Janna, and I wasn't sure when I might grow up enough to be ready for a true commitment.

Janna is very romantic by nature but she also has a tremendous amount of common sense—two traits rarely found together. Her friends constantly look to her for counseling. She has no psychology background, though you'd think she had from the way she perceives and understands people.

Our differences provide a good balance. I've been nicknamed The Computer by guys I've played volleyball with. Janna will say, for example, that when she's preparing spaghetti sauce and asks me to cook the noodles, I want to count them first. Then there's the story of a day we spent in San Francisco. I spent an hour or so in the morning making a schedule for the whole day. Where to go, what to see—with time limits at each stop. Janna is much more spontaneous, letting things happen as they will. But even she would have to admit that day in San Francisco was wonderful.

At the beginning our relationship was anything but ususal—in fact, often it was frustrating. I was busy with my final two quarters of school and immediately thereafter, in June of 1983, I joined the USA Team full-time in San Diego. My travel schedule caused us to be apart for months at a time, but we managed to endure that. Janna was really my first close girl-friend, in high school or in college. And she would be my last.

When I gave my speech in San Diego in early January, the USA Men's Team was having serious internal problems. The East-West division between players, and between players and coaches, had only gotten worse since the forming of the team in 1981. It was Californians against non-Cal-ifornians, which included the coaching staff. The guys from the West Coast gradually tightened their group—socializing among themselves off the court and ostracizing everyone else on the court.

"See you at the beach?" the California players would ask each other after practice. We never asked the coaches and only jokingly asked the Easties. First, they didn't even go to the beach. Second, they didn't play much beach volleyball. And third, we just didn't have a lot in common.

So the assistant coach, Bill Neville, had an idea to take the team on Out-ward Bound—to the Canyonlands National Park in Utah, in the middle of winter. It was supposed to be a bonding experience, a chance to build trust and respect among all the players and to break down the clique mentality.

To me it sounded like three weeks in hell. Also, I didn't want to miss another quarter of school because of volleyball. My goal was to graduate in June and then join the team full-time. That was one of the reasons that I used in order to weasel out of the Outward Bound trip, which worked to my advantage since Beal had always stressed the importance of every player finishing his education. The other excuse I had was the upcoming NCAA Scholar-Athlete dinner in San Diego—an honor not only for me, but for the sport.

Fortunately, I was told that to get the award I must be at the luncheon in January. I was the only one who had sufficient excuse to escape going on Outward Bound. A lot of the guys dreaded going and were even more upset when they came back. Chris Marlowe told me, "It was the worst three weeks of my life."

However, they did have some entertaining stories afterward. They told me that they'd had to walk with eighty-pound packs, wearing snowshoes at times, over mountain ranges. At one point the tip of one of Beal's snowshoes momentarily caught on something. When he tried to recover by running down the slope to get his feet back underneath him, he ended up face-planted in the snow with all the guys laughing at him. It was on a steep slope, and with the heavy pack, he couldn't get up. But before giving him some help, the players made him wait while they snapped photos of the scene.

The cold was terrible. They woke up to frozen boots. By the time they arrived at the airport for the flight home, they hadn't had a shower in three weeks. Their bodies were reeking and they kept apologizing to people on the plane.

As for accomplishing the goal, the players who were my closest friends told me that they didn't come out with any more confidence in certain guys on the team than they'd had before. In fact, less in some cases. Being on the volleyball court with certain players was bad enough, but to have one of them as your partner in a life-threatening situation—like climbing a sheer rock face—was pretty scary. From all accounts I heard, no new bonds were formed. I was thrilled to have been able to stay home in the safe and warm classrooms of UCLA. We would have to figure out some other way to build unity on the team, but we weren't sure we'd ever succeed.

The NCAA Scholar-Athlete award capped off my collegiate career at UCLA. My fourth and last year, in 1982, was another memorable one. For the second time, we went through an entire season undefeated. When you play on a team that never loses, there are a lot fewer problems than normal.

It was a good group of guys and loaded with talent. Dave Saunders was on that team and he would go on to play on both the 1984 and 1988 Olympic gold-medalist teams. Ricci Luyties was a sophomore that year as was Doug Partie. Both of them played on the 1988 Olympic team, and while playing at UCLA they were on four NCAA championship teams—the only two starting volleyball players to have ever done that.

I remember that year for another incident—one that I'll never forget. I rarely let fans or hecklers distract or unnerve me. In fact, I love competing in front of hostile crowds like in Brazil or in Italy. Most of the time I don't even hear what they're saying. But this time I did, and it involved a fan who was a paraplegic.

In 1982 Ricci Luyties had become our other setter, but in midseason a knee injury forced him to undergo arthroscopic surgery. So now I had to set a 5–1 system, which I had never done before. I didn't consider myself a good setter but somehow we kept sneaking out wins. That era was marked by our great battles with USC, and this particular incident happened in the old Trojan men's gym. As usual, the little gym was packed and noisy, and the USC fraternity brothers were in the upper section with a keg of beer and getting rowdier as the match went on.

There was also a small section for disabled people, on the floor right near us. One guy in a wheelchair was taunting me the whole match. If USC scored a point, he'd roar, "How do you like that 5–1 now, Karch!" I just kept setting Dave Saunders the whole match and he won the match for us almost by himself. But the guy in the chair was relentless. I couldn't block his voice out and it was really getting to me. As soon as we won the close fifth game, I didn't even celebrate with my teammates. I sprinted over to the guy, got right in his face, and screamed, "How do you like that f***in' 5–1 now, baby!"

He was pretty blown away. Remarkably, I ran into him a few months later in Westwood. We chatted and, although he felt I overreacted a little, he appreciated not having been treated with kid gloves—and I certainly hadn't treated him with kid gloves. In fact, I took them off and hit him as hard as I could, verbally. But we both understood that he was in his Trojan mode and I was in my Bruin mode, and it was competition.

Since we won our league in 1982, we were already qualified by the time the NCAA Regionals came around in May, and all of us Bruins decided to go to watch the match in Los Angeles. Some of us drank a few beers before the match and started heckling the Trojans—I figured it was my turn to do some friendly jeering. Not only was it in poor taste, but it served to fire them up. They had been losing early to the University of Hawaii, and it may have been our taunting that helped them turn the match around.

The Final Four was at Penn State, and when the teams attended the pre-tournament banquet we saw that the USC guys were furious at us for our heckling at the Regionals. It was obvious that they were dying to play us, so they must have been looking past Penn State in their first match. Penn State beat them in a huge upset. The next night we smoked Penn State, 3–0.

Steve Timmons was on that USC team. By that time I'd gotten to know Steve better. I went to some USC parties with him after matches. During my last two years at UCLA, I partied much more than I had in the first two. I really don't know why, but some of us at UCLA were pretty out of control—a lot of volleyball parties and a lot of beer drinking. "Quarters" was a popular drinking game in which one particular guy can be picked on. Players sit around a table and take turns trying to bounce a quarter off the table and into a glass of beer. When someone succeeds, he gets to pick who chugs the glass. It seemed I got picked on a lot. I can't believe how stupid and destructive that behavior was, and what a poor example I set. At least I figured it out—some people never do.

After school ended in June, I rejoined the USA Team in San Diego. We started the 1982 summer with a six-week trip to the Orient. Before that, our longest trip was two weeks—that fateful trip to Japan the year before. Now we were off for two weeks in China, two in Japan, and two in Korea. Japan was a real measuring stick for us and we won three out of seven matches.

Throughout the trip guys were getting sick, mostly with stomach ailments, but otherwise it was a pretty good experience. The younger, single guys didn't mind the traveling as much since they had less to be homesick about and all our expenses were paid. At home we were getting zilch—not even living expenses.

That trip had been in preparation for the 1982 World Championships in Argentina—a big event for us. Part of the preparation was meetings with sports psycholgists where we sat down and selected goals for the next three years. The goal in 1982 was to get fifth or better in the World Championships. In 1983 we wanted to earn our way to the Olympics—not by default, since in Los Angeles we would have an automatic berth as the host country. That meant beating the Cubans in the NORCECAs. Our goal for the 1984 Olympics was to win a bronze medal or better.

Some older, former USA Team players had rejoined the team in 1982. Jon Roberts and Jay Hanseth had played in the IVA pro league, which folded in 1980—both had gotten their eligibility back after the FIVB changed its ruling on ex-pro players.Chris Marlowe, who had been trying to break into acting, also came back to play.

The trip to Argentina was ill-fated from the start. It was a hellish ordeal just to get there, requiring several plane connections to reach Buenos Aires. Then, instead of taking an hour flight to Catamarca where our first pool of play was scheduled, we ended up taking a nine-hour bus ride snaking up and down mountain roads to arrive in a small, uninspiring city in the middle of nowhere. That was the beginning of a disaster—the worst experience of my indoor career.

In our first practice Marc Waldie, at that time a starter, sprained his ankle. Looking back from today's viewpoint, it's strange to see how one player's injury so discombobulated us. However, we were that fragile. It was also intimidating to go to Argentina right after the Falkland Islands War. Fans threw eggs, D-cell batteries, tomatoes, and other things at us since they assumed we were sympathizers of the British—their enemy in the Falklands conflict.

We played Bulgaria the first night, a team ranked in the top ten of the world. In that international competition, teams were grouped into pools of four. Each team plays the other three and they advance according to their finish in the pool. In Catamarca only the top two teams out of four would advance to the upper bracket of twelve teams. That was essential for us to reach our goal. Since the Soviets, who had the best team in the world, were in our pool, we assumed we would lose to them. We were right. So we needed to finish second by beating the other two teams—including Bulgaria.

We were very inexperienced compared with teams from the other top countries. I remember Jay Hanseth, who was older than the rest of us and had played against many of the world's best in the IVA, noting how slowly our coach adjusted to opponents' tactics. For example, Bulgaria kept running a back quick set that was giving us fits. A quick set, coming out of the setter's hands right above his head, makes for a standard attack in volleyball. But when the attacker approaches from behind the setter—in this case, the right side hitter—it can make the attack more difficult to block. Especially if your blocking system isn't prepared for it, and ours wasn't against Bulgaria.

Beal had us in a "read blocking system" where we would wait on the ground, watch—or read—where the set was going, and then jump to block. Normally, we would guess where the setter was going to set the ball, then jump early to block the attack. But waiting a split second to read where the Bulgarian setter would put the ball made us late every time. They ran that play constantly and we never stopped it once.

Even with that problem, we were winning 12–5 in the fifth game. I remember one opportunity for us to score the thirteenth point. We had a free ball and ran a back-X play, where the middle hitter, Rich Duwelius, crossed behind the setter to attack on the right side. We depended a lot on Duwelius—a good player, but he could be erratic. He was prone to mental mistakes on the court, and since we were very immature and inexperienced at the time, we let those mistakes rattle us.

Rich had been putting away balls all night. Now, on this crucial play, he was hitting against no blocker and launched a ball into the bleachers. He cracked. Then we all cracked. Still, we had a 14–13 lead when Rich made another critical error. Our defense was arranged so that a designated player was responsible to get the dink—a system I didn't like because I felt it normally wasted a player, covering no-man's-land. This time though, Beal called the right defense, the Bulgarian player dinked the ball, and Rich had an easy play to make—if he had remembered to play in the correct position. He didn't. We lost 16–14.

That was a bitter defeat. We had utterly failed in reaching our goal by losing that very first match. The rest of the trip was no better. The next night we played against the Soviet Union. Even though we lost 3–0, we played well, scoring twelve, thirteen, and fourteen points against them. Those were the most points scored against them in the entire championship as they proceeded to win the tournament without losing even a single game. That was an awesome team.

So here we were, stuck in Catamarca. I was really down. My parents were there and I remember my dad trying to boost my spirits. No one was cheering for us, of course. In the Soviet match I put a couple of balls down against Alexander Savin, the best blocker in the world, and I heard my dad's lone voice yelling, "That's the way to show him, Karcsi!"

After that first pool, we were condemned to the bottom bracket. That meant we could finish no better than thirteenth, which we did. We annihilated every team we played the rest of the competition—including a couple of decent teams, like France—but it didn't mean much.

We were really depressed, looking for anything to lighten up things. Chris Marlowe was good at that. He begged Beal to put him in against Iraq—we called them the Iraqui Yakis—so Beal put him in as an outside hitter rather than in his normal position as setter. Every time Marlowe killed a ball he'd scream in that loud stage voice of his. We were just trying to get our aggressions out at that point.

After practices and matches we'd plead with Beal to stop the bus at a gelateria to get ice cream. He'd relent once in awhile. They had three sizes—something like thirty, fifty, and ninety thousand pesos. Marlowe would say, "Fill it up, baby! With the ninety. F∗∗∗ it! We're not gettin' better than thirteenth in this tournament, so I'm gonna enjoy my ice cream!"

Then almost half the team got really sick. Getting stomach upsets and diarrhea was something we learned to expect on trips, especially outside major international cities. One of the few things that cheered us up was a waiter named Victor. He was a really upbeat guy who only spoke Spanish, which nobody on the team understood. Even though he knew we were sick of the soup he served us every day, he'd still come out chirping "sopa, sopa!"

All I did was eat, read, practice, and play. During my career on the national team, I read a lot of mysteries and could often be found in my room engrossed in a John Le Carre book. Later I learned to take more advantage of the traveling. Had we been in Buenos Aires it probably would have been different, but we were in a small city with nothing of real interest.

Of course, Bulgaria went on to finish fifth, beating Cuba, which enraged us even more. Japan finished third, and we felt we were pretty even with them. Here we were thirteenth. It was a horrible experience from beginning to end. Two weeks of hell.

I went back to school in January of 1983. I had missed the fall quarter because of the Argentina trip and I still needed two more quarters to graduate. With my commitment to the USA Team, I was taking the minimum number of classes in order to maintain good grades. In June my last college final was from 11:30 A.M. to 2:30 P.M. I then had eighteen hours in which to pack, sleep, and evacuate my apartment. I was leaving for Finland at eight o'clock the next morning to meet the team. We met in Helsinki and flew on to Poland for five matches.

Poland was an eye-opener for me. I saw firsthand what my dad had known long ago—the Communist economic system just didn't work. The people in the Soviet bloc countries were always wonderfully cordial and gave us the best they had, but gristly beef, cheese, and tomatoes for lunch and dinner got tiresome after a few days. And that was the fare for "exclusive" guests. We could only imagine what the proletariat ate.

I remember that trip especially well because it was the only time my grandfather ever saw me play. My dad's father came from Hungary to Warsaw with my aunt and her husband. When they knocked on our door

I happened to be in the shower. My roommate, Aldis Berzins, who resembles me—in fact, sometimes people confused us—opened the door. My grandfather, who only spoke Hungarian, said, "Oh, Karcsi!"

Then he gave him a big bear hug. All the while, Berzins was saying, "No, Karch is in the shower!"

He and my grandmother had come to visit us in the States during the early '70s—the only other time I'd ever seen him. However, my grandmother had come earlier by herself. In that era the Communist government was very leery of letting the man of the house leave. When my grandfather was finally old enough not to be of use to them anymore, they let him come as well.

I was in junior high at the time of their visit and I remember what hot tempers they had—apparently a Hungarian characteristic. One day, all of a sudden, my dad and his father had a huge argument. They were screaming and my grandmother was crying. Shocked, I asked my mom, "What was that all about?"

She said, "I don't know. I think it was something about a banana." A banana? I just couldn't fathom the importance of it.

In Poland it was nice to see my relatives and to have them watch me play, but it was strange too because we couldn't really communicate. We sat at lunch and dinner a few times and tried using crude sign language without much luck. I never learned how they felt about my dad leaving Hungary when he was twenty-one. I always assumed it was just something he felt he had to do.

The two-week tour in Poland was also memorable for another reason. Their head coach, Hubert Wagner, had coached the Poles to an Olympic gold medal in 1976. He was really cocky. He had this huge head on his shoulders, and we started calling him "Horse Head." We found out that he was to get a bonus for every match they won and was already counting his money. When he lost some matches against us, he told his federation, "My team only lost because I was forced to play local players in certain towns instead of my normal starters. I could beat the U.S. with my junior team." So he felt he should still get his bonus. That got back to us. It infuriated us and we beat them three out of the five matches.

We even had a little fun on the court, which was a rare occurrence under Beal. Of course, it centered around Marlowe again. Sometimes he would do and say things to bug Beal, especially relating to the beach. He was older, he knew Doug better than the rest of us, and somehow, with his sense of humor, he could get away with it. In Poland, Marlowe was allowed to start one match and we won 3–0. Late in the match, Marlowe started serving skyballs, like on the beach.

"God **** it Marlowe, get rid of the beach crap," Beal screamed at him. But we actually got some points off his serve, so Doug couldn't say too much. We loved it.

Those wins in Poland were good for our morale. We returned to San Diego for more training and I was now with the team for good. A local land developer, Don Sammis, had agreed to help sponsor the team through the '84 Olympics. Many of us were living in a condo in one of his developments in Point Loma, a beautiful part of San Diego that fronts the bay. We slept in sleeping bags on the floor. About seven o'clock every morning the flight patterns of the planes at the San Diego airport would wake us up in time for practice. We didn't cook there. Eventually we were given a training table at an all-you-can-eat soup-and-salad restaurant called Soup Plantation. Steve Timmons and I set a record for eating nine meals there in five days to save extra money.

As far as earning money went, the only avenue for players was in the Olympic Job Opportunities Program. Under OJOP local employers would have to be convinced of the public relations value of supporting the U.S. Olympic effort and of having an Olympian as an employee. In return they would pay the athlete full-time pay for part-time work—every afternoon when we were in town and, obviously, no time while we were away. Securing jobs was a painstaking effort, but eventually most of the guys became employed. Dave Saunders worked at the Auto Club. Chris Marlowe and Paul Sunderland took part-time jobs at banks.

Since the USA National Team office, which was in San Diego, knew I intended to go on to med school, they found a job for me in December of 1983 as a physician's assistant at one of the local hospitals—tagging along but not doing much. At about that time I moved to South Mission Beach. South Mission was the liveliest beach in San Diego—jammed with small apartments filled with young people. The best beach players went there to play, in front of the boardwalk where skaters, joggers, and bikers passed all day long. Parties, especially during the summer, were nonstop. Steve Timmons and I rented a bedroom from a local volleyball enthusiast, Paul Gross. My parents paid for my rent and food—a few hundred dollars a month. That's all I needed to live on but it didn't allow me to do much else.

The lack of money was a constant sore point with us. We had been led to believe that we would get about $1,000 a month until an OJOP job became available and when that didn't happen, it led some players to look for other options. By 1982 my beach partner, Sinjin Smith, and his brother, Andrew, had gotten into modeling. Sinjin was in New York at times, making a lot of money. That was unacceptable to Beal. Sinjin had a choice to make: money and a nice lifestyle playing on the beach, or no money and the Olympics. By not showing up on the reporting date, Sinjin revealed his choice and removed himself from the team. His version, I think, differs— he says he was cut from the team for no good reason.

An even more key player was Tim Hovland. Hovland had a great career at USC and was also a top beach player. Mike Dodd, who had played basketball and volleyball at San Diego State, was also a top prospect for the USA Men's Team. Neither of them showed up by the deadline. They both decided to play professional volleyball in Italy— something Beal tried to prohibit by saying, "You're free to go play in the Italian league; just don't plan on ever returning to the team." Also, it was becoming very clear that decent money could be made in beach volleyball, but Beal wouldn't allow us to play on the beach either. Hovland's case was particularly crucial since he was such an outstanding player. After our dismal finish in the '82 World Championships, we thought we needed him to strengthen our team.

But the Hov always marched to the beat of his own drum. It wasn't the same as Beal's. In 1983 Beal came up with a bond plan whereby Hovland would put $10,000 into an escrow account, then get it back on a monthly basis if he behaved—and, more importantly, if he stuck it out with us through the 1984 Olympics.

Tim didn't buy it. He even got his brother/lawyer to fight the legality of the plan, and the ordeal eventually became a huge issue, which was covered by the press. But even more than the bond issue, I think it was Beal's prohibiting us from playing on the beach that scared those guys off. They wanted the opportunity to earn money on weekends when we didn't have any USA Team commitments. And playing in those tournaments was fun. I remember pleading many times with Beal to let me play to make a little money on the beach—a couple of thousand dollars to help pay bills.

Finally, I had to accept Beal's no-beach rule. I played in zero tournaments in 1983 and just four in 1984—only after the Olympics had finished. I would miss many beach seasons because of my indoor career. Beal's decision rankled me, but I had already decided that the Olympic dream was what I wanted most.

CHAPTER EIGHT

EASTIES

Let's get some beers and go to the beach," I suggested. Steve Timmons shrugged an okay. He didn't feel like talking much since it was one of the worst days of his life. It really hurt to see my roommate and best friend in pain like that. We were very close.

That day, during Labor Day weekend of 1983, started badly and only got worse. There was anxiety in the air when we arrived for USA Team practice that morning. We knew that the coaches were going to announce the nine players who were going to Moscow for the Savin Tournament—our most important competition of 1983. The team would leave in a few days.

The reason that only the top nine players were being taken, rather than the normal twelve, was that the Pan-American Games were being held at the same time in Venezuela. It was simply a scheduling problem. Since the Soviets were the best team in the world, the coaching staff opted to take our best nine to the Soviet Union. The rest would go to Venezuela, with some junior players to fill out the team. That led to disagreements because the Pan-Ams give a lot of booty—uniforms, clothes, and other articles. Some of that booty was given to us rather than to the Pan-Am team guys, and they were upset about it.

Before practice Steve and I had packed all our belongings into the trunk of my car. We were moving out of the apartment we were in, and intended to store our stuff until we returned from the trip. After that, we planned to rent a new place.

After that last practice the coaches announced the nine chosen players. Steve didn't make it. Instead he was going to the Pan-Ams. He was crushed.

Silently we walked out to the parking lot to get into my old Datsun. It was empty—robbed clean. Essentially, we had lost all our possessions. That got me down, but Steve was almost beyond hope.

So we jumped into my empty car, drove up to Newport Beach, got a bunch of beers, and drank ourselves out of his misery at a big Labor Day beach party his friends threw.

Although that was a hard moment for me because of Steve's friendship, I knew that we were getting better as a team. We had a domestic tour against Bulgaria in the spring of 1983. After our bitter loss to them in Argentina, they had become our nemesis. Pat Powers had just come back on the USA Team and his blocking was awesome. On the first play of the first match against Bulgaria, we served and Powers keyed on that same back quick set they had killed us with in Argentina. He clamped on it. He was so far over the net that his arms were parallel to the floor. That block set the tone for the whole series. We never let them up for air. In fact, we never lost to Bulgaria again during my career—over thirty matches in a row. We got them so they were just totally psyched out against us. They would never stop paying for relegating us to thirteenth place in '82.

The coaches had installed several blocking systems by now so we could adapt much more quickly to what our opponents did during a match. During the Savin tournament it was paying off—we were playing well. The tournament had two groups of teams, and after attending pre-tourney briefings the coaches said the format was like the Olympics—the top two teams from each group moving on to the semi-finals. A crossover.

When I got very sick with a serious stomach attack before playing the Soviets in pool play, they decided to rest me. With that format it shouldn't have mattered. We presumed we would meet the Soviets again in the finals. I was lying on the floor during the match, watching it. They beat us 3–1.

The next morning the coaches called a meeting. "Guys, we've made a mistake," they said. "We won't be playing the Soviets in the finals."

"What!" we screamed. They explained that there wouldn't be a crossover after all. Instead, each team kept its pool record and would now play the similarly ranked team in the other pool. Total record determined placement. We would get no more chances at the Soviets—and our one shot had been at less than full strength, with me lying on the floor watching.

We were absolutely livid. We won our next two matches, but big deal. We wanted to play the Soviets. It seemed like Argentina all over again. In our two biggest events to date, we had screwed up—in Argentina, as players on the court; in Moscow, off the court, by our coaches misunderstanding the format.

Later in the summer we played Cuba in the Canada Cup. We beat them 15–0 in the final game. It was great to thrash them, since usually we had a lot of trouble against Cuba and would have to face them—and the Soviets—in Los Angeles at the Olympics.

"Hey, I got a new Eastie test!" one of us Californians would reveal from time to time. By 1984 we had developed a battery of ten tests to determine whether a player was an Eastie or not. Of course, they were never performed—they were just tongue-in-cheek, theoretical tests that developed out of our observations of how some of the non-Californians played.

We joked about it all the time. A basic one was to have a blocker face the net, then throw a ball from behind him, into the net. The Eastie stands straight up and tries to play the ball, not giving himself much time to react to it. The Westie—from playing on the beach—knows to get close to the ground so he has more time to get the ball up.

During my entire career on the USA Team we trained at the old Federal Building in Balboa Park. Balboa Park is one of the most beautiful parks anywhere, but the Federal Building was constructed in 1915. It was cavernous, cold in the winter, hot in the summer, and the lighting was poor. The old ceiling had rafters in it. So another test was to send a guy running in one direction, then throw the ball up into the rafters. An Eastie would keep running, not thinking the ball would hit, bounce around, and come down. A Westie would wait, watch which way the ball bounced out of the rafters, then chase it down.

One of our favorite tests was created from watching Rich Duwelius in practice. It seemed that when he was blocking at the net, the ball would go straight up and invariably drop and hit him on the back of the neck—without him ever looking up. A Westie would know to look up but not an Eastie. So that became the "back-of-the-neck test."

Most of the team fell into one of those two categories, but there were a few exceptions. Paul Sunderland was an in-betweener because he was older and married and had a daughter—not single and wild as us Westies were—but he had also grown up in California and he got along well with everyone.

Another neutral guy, although in a different sense, was Chris Marlowe. Marlowe was the one who could get along best with everyone. He was like the hub and the rest of us were the spokes. He was great in any social situation. Marlowe could give a guy—even an Eastie—a hard time and still get the guy to laugh at himself, as opposed to us Westies who were so nasty at times with those other guys. In that sense he wasn't a total Westie, even though he was very Californian.

Beal didn't like the Eastie-Westie tension at all. No coach would—I certainly wouldn't have. But I think it's impossible for twelve guys to like each other all the time. Many of us were young, cocky, and immature. Some of the Westies, like Dusty, Pat, Dave, Steve, and I, would make jokes behind the backs of the Easties. Mostly they were about Duwelius, since we had no confidence that he could come through in the clutch and we felt that Beal was keeping him around because they were both from Ohio State. Looking back on it now, it's easier to see how cruel we were, and our only rationale was that we didn't want to have any weak links on the team.

If Beal didn't appreciate the Westie mentality, he got even in practice. His workouts were really tough. We would go hard for four hours and then do excruciating jump training. We lifted weights as well. Most of the training theorists today would say that our training—performing all the plyometrics and jump training after practice when we were really tired—was wrong. The experts say that you should only do those exercises when you're fresh. We were lucky that no one was seriously injured. But, in the end, we got stronger and better.

Looking back, I'm certain we needed that discipline. As much as we hated the medicine, we had to take it. We learned how to win and how to be the best. But if Beal had stayed on and driven us that hard for another four years, I don't think many of us would have lasted to the Seoul Olympics.

Away from the gym I hung out most with Dave Saunders, Marlowe, and, of course, Steve. Steve and I lived together, lifted weights together, suffered together, and partied together. When Janna and I bought a house in 1986, he continued to live with us. When we both went to play in Italy in 1989, Steve was also married and both couples lived in the same three-story apartment. We were close for a long time and he was a great friend. In 1992 we seemed to drift apart—something I'll talk about later.

A key player on the team was Dusty Dvorak. I wasn't as close to him because he was engaged and was less inclined toward partying and socializing than others of us were. Dusty's father-in-law was some sort of movie producer, and in early 1983 he put together a movie called *Spiker*. Essentially, it was based on our team but with the names changed. The plot included the player-coach tension on the team. The character based on me was known as Ketch Ficelli. There was a Tim Hovland character too, a free-spirited renegade. We were asked to be background players.

At first it sounded like fun. Better than practice anyway, and we could make a few bucks. We soon sensed that it was going to be an amateur project. One thing was for certain: It wasn't going to win any Academy Awards.

In December, Beal actually gave up two or three weeks of practice so that we could work on the movie. We had to be at the Federal Building gym from eight to noon for filming and we were paid fifteen or twenty bucks per day. Dusty's father-in-law turned out to be fairly inept. So much so, that Dusty finally had to take over—producer, director, scriptwriter, costar—which was pretty hilarious to the rest of us.

The actors weren't particularly athletically gifted. One scene took forever to film. A main character was getting punished in a drill called "coach-on-one." Here, the coach keeps hitting ball after ball at a player playing defense. The drill is designed to tire the player to the point where he can't get up off the floor. Of course, it doesn't come across on film very well when the actor couldn't even dive for a ball when he had two feet of foam padding underneath him. The best he could do was look tired. We were standing in the background, bored, and firing balls at the poor guy's back. Soon we were sick of the whole thing. It looked so lame.

Another comical scene in the picture was when the main character, who was rather short, had to use a mini-trampoline to make himself look like he was jumping higher. He would run and launch off the trampoline but they just couldn't get it right. It took hours. During the afternoons we had the option to earn fifteen more dollars for another three or four hours of mostly standing around. We did it for a few days, but it was so utterly boring that we finally said, "Forget it. We aren't that desperate."

When the movie was released we saw it in a local theater. We laughed all the way through, it was so bad. It lasted only four days in release—one of the quickest runs in history. Today it can be rented as a video. My beach partner in the Atlanta Olympics, Kent Steffes, loved to quote from it, saying, "It was so bad it was good."

Some years later, in 1990, *Sideout,* a feature film based on beach volleyball, was made. Although it starred Peter Horton and C. Thomas Howell, it wasn't much better than *Spiker.* They just had a bigger budget. Sinjin, Hovland, and Stoklos all had roles in that. I was approached to play a role but I opted out after my experience with *Spiker.* Another major reason I turned it down was that the star of the story, played by C. Thomas Howell, was a Midwesterner who comes out to California for the summer. According to the script, he gets good enough in a few weeks to beat the best players on the beach, most of whom, including me, were to play themselves. I felt too much pride about the sport, and about how much effort the great players have to expend to become great, to swallow that scenario. So I declined. I'm glad I did.

In February 1984 we took a trip to Havana, Cuba. It would prove to be a pivotal one for our team. In the first match we had a swing at match point, then went on to lose it. Duwelius was still starting and there was also still a lot of frustration when he was on the court. He made things look so effortless at times, but other times he'd just lose it for some reason. In the second match Duwelius was injured and replaced by Steve Timmons. I remember wondering how Steve would do, because up to that point he'd never been that consistent either.

But all of a sudden Timmons was killing every ball down in the front row. Then, during some scramble plays, he started calling for sets from the back row. According to the rules, a player who is in the back row can spike if he takes off from behind the ten-foot line on the court. Although it's a common strategy seen today, it wasn't used a lot at that time. Our team certainly didn't use it much. Until that night.

I'd never seen anything like it. Timmons was just blasting balls from the back court. He could broad-jump so far, sometimes over ten feet, that he was landing at the net after he attacked. It was like a front row spiker hitting a normal set, except Timmons was coming from the back row. That gave us an extra powerful offensive weapon.

In one match, Timmons became a starter. Nobody knew if he could keep this up, but the next day he did the same thing. And never looked back. In the past he had played like that for parts of a match, but never for an entire one. Now Dvorak started giving the ten-foot set to him all the time. Unlike Powers, who needed a high ball, for Timmons it was the lower the better. Timmons's attack was harder to defend because it was so fast. He normally attacked it from the right quarter of the court. This is called a "D set." My specialty was hitting a fast set to the outside left. It really split the block up, and we had Craig Buck, six-foot-nine, in the middle hitting the quick set.

We ended up 2–4 on that trip, which was two times more than we'd ever beaten Cuba in their country. More importantly, we found the last piece of our team's puzzle for Los Angeles. Prior to that we were solid in five positions, but the sixth had been inconsistent. Timmons proved that he was the guy to take the sixth spot.

Even as late as 1983 there was some interest by all of us to have Tim Hovland back because we didn't have the right combination on the floor. The sixth spot was missing. But after Timmons came into his own, I think Hovland's presence became moot because we didn't have a place for him in that particular lineup. He was a great player, no doubt, but he wasn't as good a passer as Aldis Berzins. He was a great hitter and a good blocker, but he wasn't the backrow hitter that Steve had just become. We needed the put-away punch of Powers and the great middle blocking of Buck. The other two spots were filled by Dusty and me.

Beal always told us that the best team is not necessarily the best twelve players, but the twelve who fit together the best. I didn't always agree with that because talent, too, is essential for success. In Hovland's case, Beal thought he was cancerous. I wanted him on the team because he was one of the best competitors I've ever played with or against. Unbelievably fierce. Plus Hovland and Dusty hooked up very well with the quick attack. But on the Cuba trip Steve proved that he was as good as Hovland in hitting the quick stuff. He was also a better blocker, better in the backcourt, and the best hitter from the back row. All in all, I don't think Hovland would have fit into the six as well. So Beal was right on that one—at least after Timmons came into his own.

However, in March of 1984, Beal and his staff proved to be inconsistent with Beal's own stated philosophy when he cut Marlowe from the team. Marlowe was the glue that held our team together. As soon as the coaches announced the cut, many of us went in and told them they'd made the wrong decision. They had decided to take Rod Wilde—coincidentally, an Eastie—as the second setter behind Dvorak. Some of us were very upset about the decision, and the absence of Marlowe had an immediate effect on morale. Guys began to bicker more without the one guy who could bring the team closest.

Cuba had been a turning point, but our trek to the Soviet Union a few months later was even bigger in our minds. We weren't sure which team was the best in the world. Most people felt that the Soviets were better, but we were improving fast. The four matches there would be a prelude to the Los Angeles Olympics. By now we were thinking that we could get at least a silver medal.

In the first match in Moscow they beat us 15–8. Then we caught fire and waxed them in the second, 15–2. I remember watching Craig Buck clamp down on their outside hitters, one play after another. He had a great match. Buck, at six feet nine inches, is the best blocker I ever saw. There were times when he would get so hot blocking that he could shut down a team almost by himself.

The match continued to go back and forth, and we finally won in five games. We went nuts. Afterward, we were screaming and yelling in the locker room. We were on cloud nine. What if we could do this in L.A.?

At some point that night of May 9, 1984, the Soviet boycott of the Los Angeles Olympics was announced. The Soviet government had decided to retaliate for President Carter's decision to boycott the 1980 Olympics in Moscow. Politics had won over sport again. I think Beal was told right after the match. He could have told us while we were celebrating, but he decided to wait until the next morning, letting us savor the first American victory over the Soviet Union in sixteen years—and the possibility of a gold medal in L.A.

We took it very hard. I can't even imagine how the poor Soviet guys felt—they had been the best team in the world since 1977, and now they were barred from the big one. We were in shock.

So that five-game victory was anticlimactic. In fact, it wasn't even a true victory, although I only realized that years later. Many months following the match, I read an article in the official FIVB publication stating that the Soviet team found out about the boycott right before the fifth game of that first match. Obviously, that would have affected the way they played that game—a 15–8 loss. We kind of pooh-poohed the story. In fact, for years we refused to believe it. However, with later reflection and perspective, it made more sense. The fact that Beal knew it right after the match meant their people must have known earlier.

About three years ago I read an interview with one of the Soviet players on that team. He said that they found out right before the fifth game. How close then would that fifth game have been if they hadn't found out? And would we have won it?

We won the next three matches, 3–0. The Soviets were utterly crushed—very unlike them, although I couldn't blame them. By the end of the tour, the crowd was cheering for us and whistling at their players in disapproval. Even though their fans knew about the boycott, they weren't sympathetic. Apparently they expected their athletes to compete despite the great disappointment of just having learned that they would not be going to the Olympics.

Since we wanted to gain the mental edge over the other teams, we figured it was important to win anyway. But without the Soviets putting up a fight, Beal emptied the bench during the last two matches. He still had one more cut to make. Mike Blanchard, Duwelius, and Marc Waldie were competing for two spots. At one point he put Rod Wilde in for Dusty. One of the Soviet players got a poor set close to the net and, for some unknown reason, Rod ran over to form a three-man block against the hitter. Rod, whom we called "Sparky," often seemed to be trying to do extra, flashy things on the court. He was always chipper but somehow he rubbed people—at least the Westies—the wrong way. Rod landed on the Soviet spiker's foot and broke his own leg. It was hideous. When he held his leg out straight, the broken part and his foot just hung downward.

They put his leg in a temporary air cast and flew him home. I have to give Rod a lot of credit. I think he knew his Olympic hopes were gone, but he handled his misfortune extremely well. However, we weren't very sympathetic. Rod was a nice guy who meant well, but his idiosyncrasies didn't fit with our Westie mentality. The first thing that came to our minds was, "Whoa, Marlowe could be back on the team!"

Marlowe seemed to draw the best out of all of us. Beal had said that the guys who fit together are the best unit, and that's the logic he used to get rid of Hovland. But in Marlowe's case, Beal had contradicted himself when he cut him.

The same thing happened to Mike Blanchard. Blanchard probably had the best attitude of any athlete I've ever played with. He certainly worked harder than any guy. It was so close between him, Duwelius, and Waldie in terms of ability. But when it came to his great attitude, that didn't pay off for him at all. The other two guys were from the Midwest, as was Beal, and we Californians believed that was a factor in the decision. A month before the Olympics, Blanchard was cut.

Although we were only a few days short of our return from the Soviet Union, I was ecstatic that Chris Marlowe now had a chance to get back on the team. I tried Marlowe's number a couple times but I couldn't get through—it was hard to get phone calls out of the Soviet Union because of the avalanche of calls over the boycott. Finally I called my dad in hopes that he could contact Marlowe. He did. Chris tells the story of that phone conversation best: "Chris, did you hear the news? Wilde broke his leg and if Beal doesn't f*** you over again, you'll be back on the team!"

We then played a tour in Japan and swept all three matches—the first time ever. I remember they served Berzins nearly every ball. One time he turned gray, he was so exhausted. It was almost unbelievable how he stayed on the court. That reflected the attitude that had developed on the team.

Right before Los Angeles, the coaches decided that we would spend three weeks training at Washington State in Pullman, Washington. The idea was to mimic the Olympic playing schedule hour-by-hour and to get away from all distractions. We went into isolation training and hated it. We were in dorms and infuriated to be in the middle of nowhere—just because Beal didn't want us to be distracted.

My experiences in three Olympics have convinced me that isolation is a bad idea. You need to take your mind off the competition so you don't stress out over it. If you think about it every second for weeks prior, you will blow it all out of proportion. And that's what happened up there.

We'd practice in the mornings, lie around with nothing to do in the afternoons, then scrimmage in the evenings. A lot of the scrimmages weren't very competitive because we were thinking about volleyball too much. We just wanted to get the hell out of the gym. Tensions were running high.

Finally, toward the end of the camp, it erupted. It happened at an exhibition, an intra-squad match, that we were playing in the big gym at Washington State. There were about five hundred kids who came to watch their Olympic Team. What they saw—and heard—was certainly no example of Olympic sportsmanship.

One team was made up of the three Trojans and the three Ohio State Buckeyes: Dvorak, Powers, Timmons, Berzins, Duwelius, and Waldie. The other had three Bruins: Saunders, Salmons, and me. We also had Marlowe, Buck, and Sunderland. It was another lackluster performance—since we were sick and tired of volleyball—until suddenly, in the third game, when it became the most intense match any of us had ever played. And it was only a scrimmage!

Our team had lost the first two games and was losing the third. That, combined with feeling overdosed on volleyball, had me in a funk. Then Marlowe called a play for me to go behind and hit a backset. I hit it as hard as I could. Pat Powers stuffed it straight down, off my head, and out of bounds. More humiliation in addition to their kicking our butts. The final straw came when Powers taunted and screamed at me. That was something we didn't even do to opponents unless provoked, but we were all feeling terribly frustrated.

That triggered something in me. I ended up losing it, and everybody on our team rallied around me. That was something our team did well—circle the wagons when faced with hostile crowds and opponents. The assistant coach, Bill Neville, loved that trait in our team. Beal didn't.

On the next play I asked Steve Salmons to let me stack block—a blocking strategy where I stood right behind the middle blocker and followed the ball to wherever it was set. I was hoping that Dusty would set the ball out to Powers. He did. Powers tried his favorite shot—hard cross-court. I blocked him straight down. Now it was my turn to go nuts screaming at him. Instantly, all the frustration of those three weeks exploded in all of us. Our team started to come back, and the intensity caught fire in both teams.

Next, Dusty and Marlowe started having words through the net. Dusty gave him a below-the-belt shot with, "You don't even deserve to be on this team! You're only here because Rod broke his leg!" That comment was ironic since Dusty had pled with Beal to keep Marlowe on the team, instead of Rod, a few months earlier. I think only a few players heard Dusty, but everyone heard Marlowe's stage voice when he barked, "Well, f*** you, Dvorak!"

Timmons had only heard Marlowe's comment, not Dusty's, so he went after Marlowe. Things were getting out of control and everyone on the court was screaming. I went over to apologize to Powers, hoping to calm things down. He was too pissed off to accept it. I also tried to calm Steve down by putting my hand out to him—my best friend. He refused with a "f*** you!" as well. It just kept going back and forth, the expletives flying in front of these five hundred kids. Actually, the Ohio State guys stayed out of it—that wasn't their style.

Now totally fired up, the battle between the Trojans and Bruins, plus Marlowe, continued through five games. We were up, 13–12 in the fifth, when Dusty tried one of the dumps he liked to do. Saunders was waiting for it. He stuffed it and Marlowe bellowed, "That's the best f***ing block I've ever seen, Saundo!" We finally won, 17–15. It was like winning the Olympics. I think Bill Neville was happy to see that intensity, but I heard later that Beal was concerned that the team was breaking apart—two weeks before Los Angeles.

The guy who suffered most was the referee, Gary Colberg. He had officiated all our scrimmages, and never has a referee taken more verbal abuse than during those three weeks—we were horrible to him. At the end of the camp we all took turns writing our apologies on a volleyball, but of course there wasn't enough room to express all of our remorse.

The next afternoon at the campus pool, Dusty wouldn't talk to the guys on our team. All of a sudden he was best buddies with the Buckeyes. Finally, later that day, most of us started to laugh about our blowup the day before. But Dusty seemed more sensitive to the screaming and yelling than were the other guys, and he remembered longer. Pat and I, for instance, might berate each other during a match in the midst of our competitive frenzy, then shake hands and laugh it off over dinner that night. Dusty was the greatest setter in the world, but we had to be more careful in our choice of words with him. That was probably one reason why, when Beal had us vote for Olympic team captain—Dusty had been the captain until then— we elected a new one. Chris Marlowe.

CHAPTER NINE

L.A. '84

I still get goosebumps thinking about it. The opening ceremonies of the Los Angeles Olympics was one of the most amazing experiences of my life. Unfortunately, we only got to see part of it. The last part.

All of the athletes—ten thousand of them—were taken to the Sports Arena across from the Los Angeles Coliseum before the ceremonies. On a huge screen, on closed-circuit television, we were supposed to watch the opening ceremonies along with the rest of the world. Inside the stadium were a hundred thousand spectators. Five minutes into the opening ceremonies the internal TV in the arena went down. Worse for us, we actually had a five-hour wait without seeing anything since the host country goes last in the Parade of Athletes.

That was really disappointing. On the other hand, it built the suspense. Finally we lined up to march out. The women went first, short to tall—over three hundred of them. The men were also lined up short to tall, so we were in the very back and the last to go in. Just as we were entering the back of the tunnel that led to the Coliseum, the first American athletes were coming onto the track. We felt a rumbling like an earthquake, then a blast of noise came barreling through the tunnel. The thunderous applause was almost like a hurricane—a sound wave that nearly blew us over. It kept up until we exited onto the track. A wall of sound that lasted a couple of minutes.

As soon as the American team walked onto the track, something happened that had not happened before in almost a century of Olympic history. Always before, the teams stayed in strict formation as they marched around the track. But American athletes are different—we let ourselves get swept up in the moment. We broke ranks and ran toward the stands, looking for family and friends, waving and holding up signs like "Hi, Mom." The rest of the world resented it. When it happened again in Seoul, Korea, four years later, there was even more criticism.

It was dusk when we finally got into the Coliseum. Soon the granddaughter of Jesse Owens—an Olympic track and field champion in the '30s—came running around the track with the Olympic torch. When she got near the Americans, we kept jumping onto the track to take pictures with the Kodak cameras they gave us. She barely had room to get by. Then she handed the torch to Rafer Johnson, the great Olympic decathlon gold medalist, who took it up and lit the Olympic flame. That was an unforgettable moment.

As for the competition, I started out playing well but as the matches progressed I played worse and worse. I was just out of sync. We beat Argentina 3–1, and then Tunisia and Korea, 3–0. Our last match in pool play was against Brazil. We had scouted them to death. We also knew we could qualify for the medal round without scoring a point, since Brazil had been upset by Korea in pool play.

Against Brazil I had the worst match of my entire career. It was the only time I've ever gotten benched. I stunk up the court. Fortunately, the outcome of the match was meaningless. But my play was frustrating at the same time. Beal didn't go with our normal starting lineup, putting Salmons and Sunderland in place of Powers and Buck. We were out of kilter all night and it had started with the very first play. Brazil ran a play, and their attacker hit the ball to his left rather than his right—the opposite of what the scouting report had said.

I thought to myself, "Wait a minute. Eleven out of twelve times this guy hits it this way. Now what's this?" I think we were overly concerned with what they were doing rather than playing our own game. Plus, they were blasting jump serves like I'd never seen in my life. We lost 3–0. I found out later that the Koreans were furious about our losing that match. If we had won they would have advanced to the medal round, rather than Brazil. They thought we blew it on purpose because we were more afraid of playing them than Brazil in the final round. That was untrue.

The Brazil loss shook my confidence because I had played so poorly. There was an electronic message system at that Olympics. Sinjin Smith's mom was working as a volunteer and passed on a message that Sinjin had sent to me. He said I was rushing on my attack approach. He was encouraging, and that was really nice.

A few nights later we beat Canada 3–0 to get to the finals. Since Brazil beat Italy in the other semi-finals, we would have a rematch against Brazil. In our first match against them, their jump serves were on fire. In the gold-medal finals they missed a bunch at the start. Since they were far behind in all three games, they needed to go for aces to catch up. With that much pressure, they weren't relaxed and started missing even more serves. We annihilated them 3–0. I played okay, not sensational, but everyone else played great.

After the last point was scored, Dvorak clamped on an outside set sending it to the Brazilians' side of the net. Steve Timmons sprinted to the referee's stand, climbed up on it, then jumped off. Chris Marlowe broke out an American flag and started running around the floor. It was finally over.

All that happened in front of thirteen thousand crazed fans—and millions of TV viewers. In fact, we got a lot of national television coverage throughout the Games, even though boxing preempted quite a bit of the final match. Still, much of the country knew about us winning the gold.

Movie and TV star Tom Selleck, who was our honorary captain, came into the locker room after we won. Grinning from ear to ear, he told us about almost coming to blows with a Brazilian journalist who was cheering and kept standing up in front of him. He also recounted how he had thrown away the pair of underwear he had been wearing when we lost to Brazil. Then, for good luck, he went out and bought a new pair for the Canada match, which we won. So he then wore the same ones for the finals.

The lure of a gold medal tempts some athletes to cheat, which is why every Olympics has drug-testing. In pool play one player from each team, chosen randomly, submits a urine sample. In the medal rounds two players do it. Of all nights to get selected, my number was drawn after the finals. It took me almost three hours to generate enough urine for a valid sample. Then I joined the team at the celebration at the nearby Marriott, and made up for the lost time. We got crazy that night. A lot of champagne and a lot of smiles.

My feet didn't touch the ground for the next two months. I did not feel that same euphoria in the next two Olympics I competed in. The next gold medal we won, in Seoul in 1988, was more relief than triumph, since we were expected to win. In Atlanta, when we won the gold medal in beach volleyball, I felt a sense of accomplishment, having won golds in both versions of the sport. But that first one in L.A. was such a thrill because we were playing at home, and we'd won the first gold medal ever in our sport.

On the night of the gold-medal match we didn't sleep much, if at all. Somehow we were tracked down and told that there was a meeting in the morning. Things had changed overnight. I had been planning to go to Italy to play in the pro league for six months, as many of our players did, for $50,000 to $60,000 a year. Then suddenly IMG (International Marketing Group) decided to put money into marketing our team and promoting a series of domestic tours. We were offered an equivalent salary to stay here and play. It did seem a shame to break up just as we had reached the top, so we met to discuss staying together. Our heads were buzzing with expectations.

We were still in a dream when the closing ceremonies came around a few days later. I walked over to the Coliseum with Marlowe, milling around with the spectators. We hadn't traded many Olympic pins or other mementos during the competition, but now we saw that souvenirs of the Games were hot stuff—even our little USA pins were worth thirty dollars apiece. Word of their value quickly got out to the team. Craig Buck actually wheeled his suitcase down the sidewalk, opened it up, and sold everything. Steve Salmons had left his stinking knee pads at the Olympic

Village, so I grabbed them and sold them to some memento-seeker for $10. I ended up making $700 later that night selling Olympic pins for some badly needed cash.

Right after the Olympics, Southland Corporation launched their "Victory Tour," inviting any American Olympic medalist to go on an all-expenses-paid trip around the country. The tour had been announced before the Soviet boycott and it turned out that a lot more Americans won medals than anticipated. Consequently, there were about three hundred of us who went on the tour. Southland lost their shorts, I'm sure—partly because of the large number of athletes and partly because we abused our privileges so much.

It was great to have ourselves, and our sport, finally recognized in our own country. There were times we had slept on floors to get this far, and now we were having breakfast with President Reagan and his wife at the Century Plaza Hotel in Los Angeles. Then it was on to New York, Florida, and Texas for celebratory parades. It was a nonstop party.

We were also attending to a little business. On the plane, we huddled in the back and negotiated how the promised IMG money would be distributed between us. We had been told that IMG would pay a certain amount to keep the team together, and we demanded to decide how it would be divvied up. We didn't want the USVBA to make that decision. Chris Marlowe led the discussions.

It was decided that the four who left the team would get $10,000 as severance pay. The remaining players would divide the rest according to their estimated contributions to the team. I think I ended up receiving $55,000. Timmons, Dvorak, and Powers were to get $50,000. The lowest salary paid out was $35,000.

Since the offers were commensurate with those in Italy, we accepted them. Besides, we wanted to stay together and keep playing. We still had unfinished business with the Soviets.

Dusty Dvorak decided to go to Italy anyway—the only one of us who did. It was implied by the USVBA, even then, that if you went to Italy you wouldn't be allowed to play again on the national team. We figured we wouldn't ever have Dusty back. But he was the setter who had led us to our first gold medal, and he deserved to do what he wanted.

I started playing on the beach again with Sinjin right after the Olympics. Event Concepts, the group running the beach tour, had made some changes that the players weren't happy with. A new scoring system was one problem, but mainly it was the ball—the Mikasa "Suede Spike." That ball picked up a lot of sweat and got very heavy. An all-time-great player, Jim Menges, blames that heavy ball for prematurely ending his career due to shoulder problems. The players also wanted more prize money, and felt they were underrepresented. So they had formed the AVP (Association of Volleyball Professionals) in 1983. Sinjin Smith, Kevin Cleary, Jon Stevenson, and Randy Stoklos were among the leaders who formed it.

Leonard Armato was an amateur player who was a friend of the first AVP president, Kevin Cleary, and was also an attorney. He agreed to represent the group. For my part, I was less involved since I had barely played in the previous three years.

The AVP made some immediate demands to Event Concepts. They went unheeded, so it was decided to boycott the 1984 World Championships in Redondo Beach unless the AVP got its wishes from Event Concepts. I supported their efforts. However, two top players, Jay Hanseth and Andy Fishburn, broke ranks and played. They won it easily while the rest of us picketed the tournament. Our guys felt great acrimony, calling those two guys and the rest of the players "scabs"—and worse.

In the next event, the Tournament of Champions in Santa Barbara, we decided not to strike. However, Sinjin and I drew Hanseth and Fishburn in an early round. Even my dad was surprised at my anger toward those two. Jay is a good guy but the situation had upset me. A ball that Hanseth hit in warm-ups happened to hit me, and that set me off. I started hitting warm-up balls as hard as I could, right at him. During the match there was a lot of nasty talk under the net, and those guys were ostracized for the next year or so.

That was a wild tournament. Several groups of people had buried kegs of beer under the sand to hide them from the police. The spouts were sticking out of the sand, and they poured the beer into plastic cups. Before the finals, the crowd got out of control. Then Hovland and Sinjin got into a huge feud about which ball to use. They kept arguing, so Mike Dodd— Hovland's partner—and I decided to start playing pepper. The argument went on and on, and it galvanized the crowd in a negative way. Fans started taking sides, and with the drinking it almost turned into a riot. The rally scoring system was two-out-of-three to twenty-five points. We lost the first and won the next two.

Looking back today, I'm astounded at some of the things that went on in those days. It wasn't very professional, and that caused a lot of problems. For example, on today's tour all the referees are paid professionals. However, in that era, losing teams had to ref the subsequent match. The last thing you want to do after losing a hard-fought game is to officiate ten minutes later. You're already in a bad mood. Then, if you make a bad call, players are in your face. It's a volatile situation.

Finishing third-place in a tournament was the worst of all, because then you or your partner would have to stay around and ref the finals. After taking third, all you wanted was to have a beer, then go home and sulk. That led to guys having not just one beer, but maybe four or five. Reffing inebriated doesn't work, obviously. Of course, arguments ensued about preferences in reffing. Some players refused to allow certain players to referee their games, feeling that those players "had it in for them."

There were no court balls. Everyone brought their own ball and everyone thought theirs was the best. That resulted in more arguments. It was a mess.

In those days players were still responsible for calling their own double hits, as well as their own nets. Predictably, as the prize money went up, so did the cheating. The biggest arguments resulted over the interpretation of what was a legal set and what wasn't. It was very arbitrary. Some officiating players thought that a ball had to come perfectly out of a setter's hands, without a trace of spin on the ball. Others were more liberal.

Today there are still stories—and arguments—about tournaments won and lost on a setting call.

Calling—or rather, failing to call—your own double hit or net violation was something that could also erupt into the fiercest arguments. Certainly no one hesitated to point a finger and accuse an opponent if he thought he saw him commit a violation. Not surprisingly, the degree of honesty among the ranks varied greatly. Some made the honor calls; some didn't.

I was faced with that two years later at Zuma Beach, north of Malibu. I was playing with Tim Hovland in the first-ever network broadcast of a beach volleyball tournament. It went to a double final, and we were losing 14–13 when I touched the net as I was setting the Hov. I called it on myself. Point, game, tournament. We had fought so hard to win it. I went down to the beach for a few hours and just sat, thinking. It was one of the worst losses in my life. Not because I made the call on myself for the last point— that's something I would always do—I was upset that we had lost after winning the winners' bracket.

Still, it was ludicrous to put the responsibility for making calls on players in supposedly professional tournaments. That was a referee's job. The tour was far from being professional in other areas as well. I still couldn't take any beach prize money, because it would endanger my "amateur status" for the USA Team. However, I could take money from the USA Team, provided I set up a trust fund to take the money, then withdraw funds for "living expenses."

When I looked into setting up a trust fund I discovered that it cost several thousands of dollars. I didn't have the money to pay that, so I had an unwritten agreement with the USVBA. If asked in public I'd simply say, "Yeah, I have a trust fund to withdraw living expenses." But in reality the tournament promoter would write a check to the USVBA, and then the USVBA would just write a check to me.

Back in 1985 the total prize money on the tour was about $200,000. The top tournaments paid $20,000. But the game was catching the public's eye through television. Miller Brewing saw the lifestyle of the sport as a way to promote its beer. It's funny to look at pictures of that time and see the fashion—the short, tight shorts. The idea then was to stand out, wear the wildest shorts you could. Sometimes Sinjin and I even wore metallic ones.

But styles change, and so do partners. In 1984 I played in only four beach tournaments—each with the only partner I'd had since 1979. We won them. Those were the last tournaments I ever played with Sinjin Smith.

CHAPTER TEN

DETENTE

Karch, you best player in world!" he'd say after pouring each of us a shot of vodka and handing me one. Of course, in front of all the Soviet players and many of my own, I had to down it. His name was Yuri Panchenko and he was a phenomenal player.

Then it was my turn. So I'd say, "No, Yuri. You are the greatest player in the world!" According to the rules, I'd pour two more shots out of his bottle and another toast was gulped, much to the glee of the cheering players in the hotel room.

Then he'd say, "So, we drink to both of us!" And he'd pour another. We went through that for about three hours, leaving me feeling like a wet dishrag. Another Soviet player, Pavel Selivanov, spoke English very well and interpreted for the two teams. Pavel had a taste for Western ways, wearing these huge Elton John sunglasses and acting as the party director as well.

Alexander Savin was there. Many of us respected him as being one of the best players of all time. Although I had rarely played against him, I did have that chance just a few hours before. Now I was sitting there in the same room with him and his teammates—guys who'd made up the world's best team for the past seven or eight straight years.

I felt awestruck. Socializing with those guys was a great experience, but losing to them earlier that evening sure wasn't. The match was held in Hiroshima in late 1984, and it was billed as "the Real Olympic Finals"—

obviously since the Soviets had boycotted Los Angeles. It was a dogfight, as can be imagined, but we dropped it in the fifth game, 15–12.

On one level we felt that it wasn't truly an Olympic finals since we were playing without two key players. Dusty Dvorak, our setter, had gone soon after the Olympics to play in Italy for a big contract. And we had just lost Steve Timmons on a tour in Korea prior to coming to Japan. We were playing in a really cold gym in Seoul when Steve bent down to play a low ball on defense and his patellar tendon snapped. "It felt like someone hit me with a hammer," he later told us. Suddenly we were without the most versatile hitter in the world. We still had the best outside hitter—Pat Powers could go over, around, or through any block on the planet—but against the powerful Soviets we needed our full team.

After the match we were pretty down and drinking some beers in one of our rooms when someone got the idea of going to the Soviets' rooms and hanging out. That was a novel suggestion—we'd never done any socializing off the court. Our only contact with the Soviets had been on the court, where there was a strong feeling of mutual respect. That was the one team with which no yelling under the net, or taunting, ever occurred between us.

So we put on our hotel robes and tied the cotton belts around our foreheads, samurai style, and found the Soviets' rooms. They were just sitting around, quietly drinking vodka. They were pretty shocked to see us—especially in our samurai outfits—but it quickly broke the ice. Of course, the Russian social tradition of drinking vodka was employed to the fullest, and Panchenko made sure I was the first to partake. They, like most Eastern bloc teams in that era, were fascinated with America, particularly California, and asked us endless questions. At those times I was poignantly reminded of how lucky I am to live where I do.

With only a few hours sleep, I got up with the worst hangover of my life, so wasted I actually fell back to sleep for a few minutes in the shower—standing up. We had to be down in the lobby to catch the bus to the airport at eight o'clock. My roommate, Dave Saunders, and I somehow dragged ourselves downstairs.

Not surprisingly, we were a bit late arriving. With addled heads, we looked around. All we saw were a few Soviet players with beers in hand, which nauseated us even more. But no Americans anywhere! Sprinting out of the hotel, we saw that our team was already on the bus. Beal was fuming and had actually wanted to leave us, but a couple of our players had talked him into holding the bus.

That was the first part of a brutal trip. We flew home and had less than twenty-four hours in L.A. before flying to Brazil for another tour. Since we were the Olympic champions, everyone wanted to play us. They were also gunning for us. In Sao Paulo we played before the biggest crowd in my career, over fifty thousand people. The match was held in a soccer stadium where a court had been constructed in the middle of the field—a wooden platform with a smooth carpet laid on it. When it started to drizzle, the surface became so slippery that it was like playing on ice. Somehow no one got hurt, and the Brazilian fans didn't let the inclement weather dampen their enthusiasm. They cheered their heads off as only Brazilians can.

We made our weary way home, and in early 1985 we found out that Marv Dunphy, the coach at Pepperdine University, was to become our new head coach. That news fell on happy ears for two reasons. One, Marv was a very respected coach. And two, we couldn't take much more of Beal's strict ways. However, Marv had a commitment to finish the college season, so he wouldn't be joining us until that summer.

We'd had a couple of player changes as well. Ricci Luyties, a former teammate from UCLA, and Jeff Stork, from Pepperdine, were added to the team as setters. Also, when Marv arrived for practice in San Diego, he brought Bob Ctvrtlik with him—a player who'd just graduated from Pepperdine and who would eventually take the other passer spot that would be vacated when Aldis Berzins retired after the '85 World Cup.

The difference between Dunphy and Beal was almost like night and day—and a welcome one for the team. Beal had taken us to the top through discipline and hard work. Looking back from today's perspective, we needed someone to take a strong hand and shape that cocky, brash group of guys in their early twenties. Beal was an autocrat, a general, and had kept himself aloof from us. He was also an Eastie.

Dunphy was a Californian, very personable, and was smart enough to know that he would have more success managing us, rather than controlling us. We were now older, more mature, and a proven world-class team. We didn't need a militaristic coaching style, nor would some of us have accepted it. We had alternatives now. We could play for good money in Europe—and prize money on the beach was growing.

Dunphy also knew that the veterans on the team had worked extremely hard, physically and mentally, for four years. We couldn't have continued at the same level of intensive training. He gave us more time off and worked us easier than he did the new guys on the team. With the rookies, he worked them almost as hard as Beal had worked us.

Once Beal and some of the older players retired, replaced by younger Californians, our team became a tighter group. Dunphy would allow me and a couple of other guys to play on the beach when we had free weekends. We really appreciated being given a longer leash.

In the final analysis, they were both great coaches. It took Beal a couple of years to figure out a system of play that fit our talent, but he finally did it. A large part of it, the two-passer system, had been around international competition for a long time, but Beal employed it with the same two players—Berzins and me—instead of three or four. He also added more back-row hitting with the inspiring emergence of Steve Timmons as a star. Dunphy knew enough to leave alone the system he inherited. Still, he had a tough job coming in to take over a gold-medalist team.

Although Beal was now no longer coaching, he stayed very involved in the sport at a high level. He was appointed technical director of both USA Men's and Women's teams—in effect, overseeing the programs, making policy decisions, and negotiating contracts with players. Beal proved not to be any more popular with players than he had been as coach. In his new position, he would often take a hard-ass, inflexible position with us—such as his initial policy that once you left to play overseas you could never return to the national team. In essence he didn't want us to play in

Italy, or in any foreign country, despite the fact that we could earn much more money overseas. However, his policy would prove inconsistent, as we would soon see.

Dunphy's baptism by fire was to happen right away. The Soviets were coming. IMG had arranged some domestic matches billed as the Gold Medal Tour. Obviously we wanted to play with our full Olympic team, so we were thrilled that Steve Timmons had rehabilitated his knee and would be back with us. Dusty Dvorak had just returned from Italy and asked to get back on the team. He became our starting setter on that tour—a disappointment for Stork and Luyties, who had been vying for that position during Dusty's absence. It was also a huge surprise to all of of us, given Beal's previously staunch policy forbidding such a return. The greatest irony would later come in 1990 when Beal resigned his job and went to Italy himself to coach for big bucks.

"Born in the USA" by Bruce Springsteen was the theme song blasted during the warm-ups for all four matches. It was the height of the Reagan era and patriotism was running high.

The first match was in Seattle's Kingdome before more than fourteen thousand fans. A gargantuan video screen flashed replays of every rally and, while we were marveling at it, the Soviets were so astonished that they had trouble playing. A hitter would put the ball away, then immediately look up to see himself in giant action.

The Seattle fans had the double wave going and the Soviets were cross-eyed—the big screen, the music, and all the hoopla had them out of sorts. After all, they were used to playing before fans with the stoical Russian temperament—polite applause was the loudest thing they'd hear.

The second match, in Portland, was a standing-room-only sellout. It was awesome to feel so appreciated in our home country. The third event, in San Francisco, was well-attended. But the fourth, in Los Angeles, had only a moderate crowd—an anomaly, since that was the hotbed of volleyball. All in all, the tour was successful and we took all four matches.

Still, our focus in 1985 was on the upcoming World Cup in Japan. In world volleyball there is what is called the Triple Crown: the Olympics, the

World Cup, and the World Championships. The Soviets had won the Triple Crown several times, and we had decided that was our goal. Since the Soviets had boycotted the 1984 Olympics, a true Triple Crown would mean winning the 1988 Olympics when all the best teams in the world would be there.

Soon after the Gold Medal Tour, and weeks before leaving for the World Cup, we were shocked to find out that IMG wasn't renewing their deal with the USVBA. Apparently they hadn't made enough money to continue—or had maximized what they could from the Olympic gold medal—and decided to walk.

Suddenly we were faced with huge pay cuts by the USVBA. Here we had reached the pinnacle of the sport, and the USVBA couldn't figure out how to capitalize on it. It was another example of that organization's inability to cash in on its own team's excellence. That was a frustration we all shared through much of my career with the USA Men's Team.

We were essentially told by the USVBA that a certain amount of money was now available and that the veterans should split it up as they saw fit. They didn't want to pay the new guys anything! Exasperated, we engaged John Diemer, a lawyer from Los Angeles who had been referred to me in 1984 by Denny Cline, my old assistant coach at UCLA. I acted as liaison between the players and Diemer.

We had two objectives. First, we sat down as a team and created a pay scale that we all agreed on, which was a feat in itself. We wrote every player's suggested salary on a board. The salaries ranged from $45,000 down to maybe $20,000—an average cut of $15,000. Of course, the USVBA was offering much less.

Our second objective was to get the rookies some kind of salary—guys like Jeff Stork, Bob Ctvrtlik, Ricci Luyties, and Doug Partie. We failed in both objectives.

The negotiations, after several weeks, degenerated into a boycott situation. We refused to practice with our coaches. We went into practice alone at the Federal Building every morning. Obviously, tensions were running high. Scrimmages would soon devolve into screaming matches. Then I'd say, "Enough. I'll go start making phone calls."

The clock kept ticking down as we implied to the USVBA that we were considering not going to Japan. At the San Diego airport we were literally still huddling, deciding whether or not to get on the plane. My opinion was that we should go, since I felt we still had a lot to prove as a team. Pat Powers was the most vehement against going.

I tried to convince Pat of the fact that the USVBA just didn't have the money. Sure, I agreed with him that they had let us down by not taking advantage of our Olympic success, but that was over. Besides, if IMG couldn't cash in, maybe the sport wasn't as attractive as we thought it was. Finally we decided to get on the plane—after three weeks of very unproductive prep time.

In Tokyo the World Cup's format was a straight round-robin where the top eight teams played each other, then tallied their final records to determine the finish. We met the Soviets in the second match, so the whole tournament hinged on that.

And what a match that was! Three hours and fifty-four minutes—the longest match of my USA Men's Team career. All the games were close and it came down to the fifth game. I distinctly remember being way behind the entire final game: 9–3,10–4, then 11–5. That's a long way to come back. Slowly, we clawed back and took a 14–12 lead. Then Vishislav Zaitsev, the Soviet's great setter and captain, went with a quick backset. Steve Timmons had taken a guess and keyed on that set. He roofed it for the final point.

We went nuts. In many ways it was even bigger than the Olympics because we had finally knocked the Soviets off their perch in a Triple Crown event—something the USA had never done.

Now that we had won the World Cup, we turned our sights to the second jewel in the crown—the World Championships to be held in France in 1986. However, we needed to qualify for that tournament by winning our zone championship, the NORCECAs, which was to be held in the Dominican Republic. That turned out to be very memorable for many reasons.

We arrived in Santo Domingo in September of 1985. When we got to our dorms we found that they were still being built. What we were presented with was some walls, a cement slab, and no running water.

Thank God it rained every day. We would stand outside under the gutter spout and use it for a shower. For sleeping, we made do by taking the mattresses from the horrible beds in the rooms and putting them on the floor.

"Cuba si! Yanqui no!" was the familiar cry we heard when we met Cuba in the finals. The crowd was very pro-Cuban—as was usually the case when we played in Latin America—and it was incredibly hot and humid in the gym. At the time, Dusty Dvorak was still our starting setter, but his grandmother had fallen ill and so he chose to stay home. Jeff Stork was in his place as setter.

Things started well for us and we were up two games to one, when early in the fourth game Stork suddenly disappeared from the court. The only player on the court who had seen Stork leave was Pat Powers, who had sprinted off the court after him. We looked over and saw Powers near our bench, screaming at Stork, "Get out there! You've gotta play!"

Powers thought that Stork couldn't take the pressure of the match and simply folded, unable to play. What had actually happened was that Jeff had lost so much water that his body went into full body cramps— he was contracted into a ball. We knew that Jeff sweated a lot, but in that sweltering gym, water was actually sloshing up and out his shoes, leaving reverse footprints wherever he walked. If he dove for a ball, the floor got soaked. We came to call him Lake Stork, and after that he'd bring two sets of shoes and three complete uniforms to play a match.

Dunphy ordered Powers back on the court and quickly substituted Dave Saunders in the game. Saunders had never set, so the six of us were standing there in utter confusion. Who was setting?

Suddenly Dunphy yelled: "Karch, you're setting!"

I hadn't set in years but I had no choice here. It was shaky from the get-go. Obviously we were screwed up without Jeff, and our lead began to slip away. I put some high sets up to Powers but they weren't as accurate as Stork's. Powers screamed at me, "Get the ball closer!"

"Just hit the f***ing ball!" I screamed back.

Finally I started setting every ball to Saunders and Timmons, who were near to me in the rotation and a little easier to set. They began hammering away, and we started rolling. The Cubans, who thought they had the match iced when they saw Stork go down, were getting tighter and tighter as Saunders and Timmons caught fire. As we climbed back, Cuba got more frustrated and we somehow took that fourth game, and the match, 15–11. It was perhaps the most amazing match of my life because we won playing with a lineup that we had never practiced before, and never used since.

After the match we found out that Stork had been taken to the hospital and that it took several IV bags to get him rehydrated. His life was actually in peril, he was so dehydrated.

So 1985 was a big year for the USA Team. We had made strides toward our Triple Crown goal but, more importantly, we had done it by overcoming serious adversity.

The year 1985 was also big for beach volleyball in this country, but for different reasons. In the summer of that year Playboy ran a feature on Tim Hovland. Called "Volleyball Gods," it characterized the dissipated lifestyle of a pro beach volleyball player—a racy tale of countless beach babes and a lot of drinking. I don't know how much was truth and how much was not. I do know that Tim thought it was an unfair characterization, and he felt that he had been misled by the writer.

I also know that there was a lot of partying on the AVP Tour in those days. It was the era of the bikini contests—Miss Miller Lite or Miss Hard Body (sponsored by Nissan Trucks). Here were these shapely women, strutting around in scanty bikinis, in front of good-looking players looking for fun. Liaisons, of whatever sort, were predictable.

There were also plenty of beautiful women who were not entered in the bikini contest who seemed to be vying for guys'—especially the players'—attention. That was the time before bleachers, so you could set your chair anywhere that you chose on the beach. Some of the girls would get to the tournament early so they could set their chairs right near center court. Of course, they'd have to get up every fifteen minutes to parade through the whole crowd to get a drink of water, or go for a swim, then sashay back.

In the early '80s, part of a player's obligation was to help promote the AVP Tour by appearing at local bars to mingle and get fans out for the tournament. These events were usually arranged by the local Miller or Cuervo distributors. Sometimes the prelims for the bikini contests were held on the Friday night at these functions, and some of the top players were judges.

They could be wild and crazy affairs, but since I hardly played on the beach during the early '80s, I wasn't around very often for the festivities. In the second half of the decade I played somewhat more, but not much. Five tournaments in '85, half-seasons in '86 and '87, and one tournament in '88. My commitment to the USA Team still took precedence.

Not that I didn't enjoy myself when I had the chance. After a few beers with friends following tournaments, I enjoyed dancing but I certainly wasn't one of the Volleyball Gods. After all, I was with Janna from 1983 on, and I took that commitment seriously.

Before I met Janna I was unattached, and hanging out at beach parties was the normal thing to do. In fact, partying had always been a part of beach volleyball tradition. For decades, players had prided themselves on drinking on Saturday night as much as on playing on Sunday. That was a common phenomenon that happened in all sports before the current era of professionalism. But just as in other sports, the partying decreased with the increase in salaries. Simply, the stakes got higher.

In about 1992 the bathing suit contests were abandoned by the sponsors because of changing social consciousness and because of the perception that they diminished the seriousness of our sport. I never was a great fan of the contests because they would literally stop the tournament for two hours on Saturday, so their cancelation didn't bother me. But some players were disappointed—especially the guys who served as judges and enjoyed the extra-close exposure to the contestants.

I've always found the issue of dealing with the women easy—I don't. I send out this aura that I'm not interested, because I'm not. I'm totally committed to my wife and kids.

I'm aware that some guys on the tour play around on their "loved ones." I don't approve of it and I don't respect them for it. Some guys think the grass is always greener, and they'll never stop looking elsewhere. For me it's pretty simple. It's just not worth jeopardizing what I have with Janna. She's so beautiful—on the inside and on the outside. She's the best thing that ever happened to me. Why look elsewhere?

Nowadays I'm kind of a hermit on the tour. I play, I eat, and I might do a couple of promotions or autograph sessions during the weekend, but otherwise I spend my time in my room. It's that way for most of the players. With more prize money, the players' routines have become much more conservative.

"Karch, would you like to participate in the *Superstars*?" It was a television producer from ABC on the phone.

I almost dropped it. "Uh, sure! When is it and where?"

"In South Miami Beach. Starts next Wednesday." And this was Friday night.

I agreed to go, hung up, then began wondering how I was going to pull it off. After all, I was in Brazil when I got that phone call in February of 1985—on a USA Men's Team tour. Our team departed Brazil Sunday morning and arrived in L.A. late Sunday night.

The next morning I took a golf lesson from Janna's dad in San Clemente. I'd never played a round of golf in my life. Still, I figured that it was one of the events I might have a long shot at. He instructed me on how to make an easy swing with a six-iron. In the Superstars I'd have three swings at the hole 150 yards away.

Next I drove the two hours up to UCLA for a quick weightlifting lesson from strength coach John Arce. After that I got into the pool with Ron Ballatori, the UCLA swim coach.

He took one look at my kick-turn and said, "Don't ever try another one of those again—just touch the wall and push back off." The one I had tried sent me swimming sideways, so he was right.

Janna and I took a red-eye flight to Miami that night and got in early Tuesday morning. At the hotel there were famous athletes roaming around the lobby—TV celebrities such as Olympic boxing great Evander Holy-field, Heisman Trophy winner Hershel Walker, and track and NFL star Willie Gault. Being a humble volleyball player, I was considered low man on the totem pole—consequently, they didn't have a room for us. We were dead tired, so we just took our suitcases out on the beach, found a palm tree, and took a nap—using my suitcase for a pillow.

Later in the day we finally got a room. I went over to the obstacle course to check it out, since that was the most famous event. You have to pick seven out of the ten possible events to compete in, so I decided not to compete in the rowing, the bowling, or the golf. My one golf lesson hadn't given me enough confidence.

The prelims, consisting of two separate groups of athletes, lasted two days and I won my division. I won the swimming event—even without a kick-turn. And I won the tennis. But my winning the weightlifting was an utter shock. John Arce at UCLA had taught me a bit of clean-and-jerk tech-nique. In essence, he taught me how to employ the jerk—using my legs to hoist the bar from my shoulders to above my head. The pro football play-ers would just stand there and lift the weight with only their arms because they were so strong. Using my legs I got 260 pounds up, which didn't sit too well with the humongous NFL players. They didn't seem to appreciate this puny volleyball guy beating them in a strength event.

I did pretty well in the half-mile run and ran a 10.8 in the 100-yard dash, which got me some points as well. However, I bombed in the bicy-cle race. It was on a flat track and I was too afraid to cut an aggressive line. The problem was that I had seen some ugly crashes on TV in earlier *Super-stars*, and I didn't want to end up a casualty.

Winning my division, I got to move on to the finals after a day of rest. It also meant I'd win a huge amount of cash—at least $10,000. I had only been earning money from the USA Men's Team for about four months.

For the finals there were ten athletes competing. I switched out of the cycling and obstacle course and into the rowing and golf because of my fear of crashing and burning. I started well, winning the swimming and the tennis. I have to admit that I hadn't played much tennis, but my volleyball helped a lot. I found myself charging the net, jumping as if to spike, and killing a lot of balls. Fortunately, no one was very good at lobbing the ball.

In the finals of swimming someone jumped the gun, but for some reason they didn't whistle a false start. So there I was, standing on the platform waiting for the recall, and the field was in the pool and gone. I realized in a panic that the false start wouldn't be called, so I dove in and took off. I think I took one breath down the length of the pool and one breath on the return. Somehow, I barely nudged the leader to win. In the post-race interview, I was so out of breath that I couldn't even talk.

In fact, I was really nervous the whole time. It was no fun putting so much pressure on myself. My feeling was that this was a great opportunity to represent volleyball players and to prove how we could measure up against athletes in major sports. As contrived as the *Superstars* is—and certainly not a perfect measure of athletic skill—it was still the only test of its kind, and I felt like I was carrying the weight of the whole volleyball world on my shoulders.

In the weightlifting finals I got third. The great NFL defensive end Marc Gastineau lifted something like 330 pounds—using just his arms. I could see that the *Superstars* title was coming down to him and me. On the final day, I had to go first in the golf—a mandatory event for the finals—which was a shot over a lake. I actually hit three decent shots—total luck. The first two hit within about fifty feet of the pin and the third about thirty-five feet from it, which put me in second place.

The last guy to go was Gastineau. It was obvious that he wasn't a golfer either when he ripped his ball about 300 yards straight right. His second ball, a 300-yard hook to the left, put him dead last. Since I was sitting about thirty-five feet from the pin, only a shot short of a miracle would prevent me from finishing second in the golf—and, as I would find out later, cinching first place overall. Gastineau lifted his third shot over the lake and it landed about two feet inside my ball!

Suddenly, Gastineau went from last to second in the golf and put me in third place. Then came the half-mile. I was still in good contention but

I had to do very well in my final events to have a chance to win the whole thing. Before the race, I was as nervous as I've ever been. In the prelims I had lost to Evander Holyfield, but in the finals I overtook him in the stretch and beat him. I ran a 2:06 and almost killed myself.

At that point I took the lead by one point ahead of Gastineau and it kind of freaked out the other athletes—and probably ABC too. I had the impression that they were all wondering, "How can this be? Volleyball players are supposed to be sissies."

It came down to the 100-yard dash a few minutes later. Willie Gault, who was not only a great football player but was also a star sprinter in college, just smoked everybody. Of course, Hershel Walker could fly too. Not having their speed, I still ran a decent time for me—a 10.8. But Gastineau ran a 10.3. Imagine getting hit by a guy with a six-foot-six, 275-pound frame who could run that fast! That time got him fourth place and two points, while my fifth place earned me a single point. So we tied for total points.

"Why is he celebrating?" I asked myself. I looked over at Gastineau right after the race and noticed he was jumping up and down with glee. Obviously he already knew the rule about ties—something no one had bothered to tell me. In that case, it was decided by how the two tied athletes had done head-to-head in same events. He had beaten me more than I had beaten him.

For finishing second I won about $30,000, which was an astronomical amount of money for me. I was so close to winning it all. If it hadn't been for that one golf shot . . .

CHAPTER ELEVEN

POLITICS...AND SPORT

Pat Powers put it best. When introducing his beach teammate he would say, "This is my future ex-partner."

Beach volleyball is a little like a marriage—a doomed one. I don't think there's ever been a team that didn't break up at some point or another. It's inevitable. The top teams tend to stay together because they know they have a chance to win each weekend. However, as soon as they are knocked off their perch, they begin acting like unhappy spouses. Their analysis is pretty subjective, of course, and invariably the same: Both players think, "My partner's stinking up the court lately."

If two partners are of different age, the younger will gradually surpass the older as he loses his edge. In time the more youthful player will develop a roving eye. As you go further down the list on the AVP Tour, the players' partner-swapping gets so frequent that relationships resemble a swinging singles club more than they do a marriage.

After a weekend event, a flurry of calls starts as early as Sunday night or Monday morning in an effort to find a better combination for the next weekend. The irony is that it takes time and patience to build great teamwork. If teams fall into slumps, they too often break up rather than waiting it out.

There are many factors involved. I prefer playing with a right side player since I grew up playing on the left. Size is also a consideration. A small guy usually looks for a tall blocker to play with. At six feet two inches, I'm mid-sized, so I prefer to play with a similarly sized partner. That way we can share responsibilities evenly and prevent fatigue. If one player gets all the serves or has to block every ball in a tournament, he's going to tire more quickly. Evenly matched players, in size and skill, tend to eliminate that problem.

In 1985 my situation was a little different. The AVP was really starting to take off and I wanted to be a part of it, both for the money and the fun. Yet, even with Dunphy allowing me to play when I had free weekends, it still wasn't enough. The very top players wanted to stay with the same partner for an entire season.

That year Sinjin Smith and Randy Stoklos had solidified their partnership, which would come to dominate the AVP Tour for several years. I played five tournaments with Mike Dodd. He agreed to play with me when I was available and with Tim Hovland when I wasn't. That was fine with me but not with Hovland. He wanted to have Dodd as a full-time partner and so he gave him an ultimatum. Dodd committed to a full-time partnership and the other great doubles team of the '80s, one that had first formed in '81, was locked up.

That was the beginning of my most frustrating period on the beach. I would spend the next five years going through a merry-go-round of partners—seeking but never finding the combination that would knock Sinjin and Randy off their perch. Soon I teamed up with Ricci Luyties. We played pretty well but too many frustrating second places made me look for the elusive perfect partner. I tried John Hanley, Brent Frohoff, Leif Hanson— even my indoor teammate, Steve Timmons—before going back to Luyties. One win with Dodd in '86, none in '87, and one at a non-AVP event with Luyties in '88 were the only ones I could muster.

As the AVP Tour prize money and number of events grew, so did my frustration. It was very clear now that the top players were going to stay with one partner for an entire season. Money had brought a new sense of fidelity to the concept of marriage in beach volleyball partnerships. Also, I was getting some big offers to go to Italy to play—for far more money than

I was getting on the USA Team. It was an enticing situation: play in Italy in the winter and on the beach in California in the summer.

I talked to my agent, Jerry Solomon of ProServ, Inc., about it. He encouraged me to stay and play in the '88 Olympics, believing that if we won another gold medal we would establish a true volleyball legacy in this country. I really was tired of the indoor grind, the long workouts in the gym, and above all the endless traveling—five years running I counted over two hundred nights when I slept in a bed other than my own—but Jerry's logic was persuasive and I decided to stay and go for it. We still had the two final parts of the Triple Crown to win.

Marriage was a good analogy for beach volleyball, and marriage was also on my mind in the summer of 1986. On a night in August, Janna and I were sitting on the bed when I suddenly said to her, "Janna, I'm really nervous because I don't know how to say this . . ."

Her startled eyes told me that she was bracing herself for something terrible—as if I was going to tell her that there was someone else. I had always been intimidated by the permanence of it all. Even though I knew that I wanted to be married to just one person for the rest of my life, the reality of it scared me. But I'd finally made a firm decision, and that night I asked Janna to marry me.

She accepted. On her finger I slipped a paper ring that I'd just made out of a blank check I had rolled up. Right after my proposal, I left for the World Championships in Paris. Since I was traveling so much with the Men's USA Team, Janna made most of the wedding arrangements.

"You look like you could use a beer," said Steve Timmons, my best man, about an hour before the wedding a few months later, on December 27. He went to find one, and while trying to sneak it into the San Clemente Presbyterian Church he was intercepted. I had to go it alone. For two hours before the wedding I had actually been hyperventilating. I'd never been more nervous in my life. While reciting my lines, I got caught on "for richer or for poorer," mumbling something unintelligible. But I got through it, and walked out of the church knowing that Janna was the woman I wanted to spend the rest of my life with.

Politics is a big part of amateur sports—too often to the detriment of it. Of course, I'd seen its presence throughout my career and heard about its history in American volleyball, but I never knew how strong it could figure at the international level. I got a huge dose of it at the World Championships in France in 1986.

Representing the second part of the Triple Crown, we had to win that competition to realize our quest. Earlier in the summer we had lost at the Goodwill Games in Moscow. The '86 Goodwill Games were the first ones ever held, and we dropped the fifth game to the Soviets, 15–12. It was a bitter loss. I was the only guy to go to the Soviets' rooms after the match. Since we had started that tradition of socializing after our battles, I wanted to keep it going. We shared some beef, some tomatoes, a couple shots of vodka, and then I left.

The loss in Moscow made the World Championships even more important in our minds—we still hadn't been able to totally usurp our nemesis to become the world's reigning volleyball power.

In important international competitions every advantage is given to the host country to do well. In this case, France was put into their first pool with two very weak teams, assuring that they would advance. The remainder of the tournament was designed to give them the least amount of resistance to their arrival in the finals. A home country in the finals means bigger crowds, more TV, more money. Is it fair? Is it an example of the Olympic ideal? Hardly. But it's reality and, of course, corporate sponsorship and TV money keep amateur sports alive.

In the past we felt that the French team considered themselves a little better than they really were. They displayed a kind of arrogance—they were snooty, cocky, and had the habit of growling through the net—but with no results to back it up. Consequently, we always took a little extra pleasure in tromping them.

After the French team rolled through their preliminary pool waxing teams like Algeria and Afghanistan, they were touted in the French media as though they were heroes of the French foreign legion. We would flip through the TV in our rooms to see them on the nightly news, running around the arena after a convincing victory over a minor Third World country, throwing their jerseys to the adoring crowd. Until a few nights later when they finally had to face a real team—Brazil. In that critical match, France had a 14–6 lead at match point in the fourth game, with eighteen swings to win, and couldn't put it away. It was one of the all-time gags in international volleyball.

It didn't get much better for the Frenchmen the rest of the tournament. The noose around their necks kept getting tighter as they dropped more important matches and finished far lower than they, or the French press, expected—in sixth place. There would be no parade down the Champs Élysées for them and we certainly didn't mind.

In contrast, we had a tough preliminary pool. Since so many of the weak teams were put on France's side of the bracket—to maximize their chance of getting to the finals—our side was full of good teams. We had to beat strong teams from Argentina, Japan, Poland, and Cuba to qualify for the semi-finals. In those semi-finals we hammered Brazil 3–0, while the Soviets won their semi-final match, setting up the predicted finals.

The finals were held at a huge arena in Paris called Bercy. In Paris we were under very tight security since there had been a spate of recent terrorist bombings. Our bus to and from matches was led by a band of nutty police escorts on motorcycles. With sirens blaring, they would speed through the crowded streets, literally kicking cars as a signal to get out of the way.

It was awesome to play that match at Bercy with over fifteen thousand spectators. We had been on a mission for five years—to get to the top—and here was a necessary test we had to pass. Early in the match Bob Ctvrtlik got into some trouble and Dave Saunders was subbed in for a spell. Bob soon returned and our play steadied out.

Then some strange things happened. As we got better, the Soviets uncharacteristically showed their frustration on the court. We later found out that the coach, Vjatcheslav Platonov, was feuding with the team, but internal problems had never before surfaced during the Soviets' play. Later in the match Platonov made a surprise move when he subbed out their floor leader, Vishislav Zaitsev. I didn't see it, but Zaitsev stormed to the bench, grabbed a clipboard, and threw it to the floor. Those were actions rarely, if ever, seen. At the same time, it fed our confidence and we put them away 3–1. The second part of the Triple Crown dream was ours.

Then came the politics. Right after the finals of these prestigious international events, the protocol calls for a formal closing ceremony where speeches are made and awards are presented—both team and individual. Since we were in France the ceremony was done in French. None of us could understand what was being said, but when we saw the various players walking out to receive individual awards we sensed that something was amiss.

How right we were. The individual awards had been determined by the French journalists. As they announced the top six players we grew more and more confounded. Somehow they named a Soviet guy for best hitter. That alone wasn't overly disturbing, except that the player they picked wasn't even a starter! When a short Bulgarian player was announced, we figured it must be for best passer. Wrong. They named him best blocker.

Then it got even more outrageous. Although experience had taught us not to expect too much in these ordeals—even if our team wins it—having just one of our guys named to the all-tournament team seemed a bit much. It was good to see Bob Ctvrtlik chosen as best passer, but the last two picks had our mouths dropping to the floor. For the best setter of the tournament, the pundits of the press gave the award to Alain Fabiani, the French setter from a team that finished in sixth place. Mon Díeu!

The final and most prestigious accolade—Most Valuable Player— could have been given to any one of our starters, but by now we were feeling a little nervy about it. And rightly so. The MVP of the World Championships was given to a French player, Phillipe Blain. That was like giving the MVP of the NBA Finals to a guy whose team lost two rounds earlier—and to a mediocre player at best. But this was France, and homering at its finest.

Anyway, the fiasco was not lost on the Federation Internationale de Volleyball. The selections in Paris were so outrageous that the FIVB quickly decided to initiate the practice of giving its own annual award for the world's Best Player and Best Coach—as decided by themselves, and based on statistics. In 1986, the first year of that award, the coaching title went to Marv Dunphy. I was given the MVP, although I think any one of us could have legitimately received it. In 1988, after the Seoul Olympics, the FIVB named me again as recipient of the honor.

The bottom line: The French episode left us laughing, not steamed. We would have chosen a team victory with no individual awards over no victory and all individual accolades every time.

By 1986 FIVB president Ruben Acosta, a very perceptive and shrewd man, had his eyes on the burgeoning phenomenon of beach volleyball. Although he'd only been in office two years, he had already studied the Southern California scene as well as the millions of dollars that corporate sponsors were pouring into it. He also knew that it was happening in Brazil, although not on the same level. Unlike the people who ran American volleyball, Acosta wisely considered the beach game to be genuine volleyball—just a different version. The most powerful man in the sport didn't take long to realize that the sexy lifestyle image might prove even more attractive to TV and sponsors on a worldwide level than had the traditional indoor game.

In 1987 the first World Beach Volleyball Championships were held in Rio de Janeiro. It was an outrageous affair.

Sinjin Smith and Randy Stoklos at the time were dominating the AVP Tour, so the FIVB invited them down to play in the event. And to capitalize on our USA Men's Team reputation, they invited Pat Powers and me down as a team. I actually would have preferred Brent Frohoff or Ricci Luyties as a partner, but they wanted Powers as my partner because of his indoor renown.

When we arrived in February we found that some more politicking was going on. The tournament directors had made sure that our two American teams would play each other in the semi-finals, thereby assuring that a Brazilian team would make the finals. Although the best Brazilians have since improved to the level of our top players, if not better, at that time their best team was inferior to our two American teams. We didn't like it, but then again, it was good for the tournament and, after all, we were in Brazil.

There were some classic matches. Pat and I played okay but we lost to Sinjin and Randy in the semis. When one of our teams wasn't playing, we would be scouting and encouraging the other team. Quite paltry encouragement when you consider that the stadium erected on the beach of Ipanema held ten thousand screaming, singing, dancing Brazilians.

February is the height of summer—and Carnival—in Brazil and the heat is brutal. One day I saw the temperature, which is electronically posted in the streets of Rio, at 44 degrees centrigrade—that's over 111 degrees Fahrenheit. Inside the stadium, the fans were so crammed together that they blocked any hint of a breeze.

At about three o'clock in the afternoon—the hottest time of day—Sinjin and Randy were set to play Bernard Rajman and his partner, whom they called Edinho, in a late-round match. Besides the heat, we had to contend with international rules. By the end of the tournament all four of us had done a pretty good job of adapting. We had to.

The first big change included loosening the interpretation of a legal set—rarely were violations called for sets that came out of a player's hands, no matter how much they spun. Next, the rules permitted open-handed dinks, whereby a player could essentially slam dunk an attack like in the indoor game. That gave the attacker a great advantage since the court was being covered by only two defenders.

In Brazil, Bernard was a god—an indoor legend and a great beach player too. He was also a showman and knew how to use those rabid ten thousand fans. One thing he did was to serve a towering skyball that the media named "journada de estrella," or journey to the stars. He had everybody so fooled with that thing, but for us Californians it was the one serve we wanted to see because it gave us so much time to pass the ball. Bernard would turn his back to the net and fire a top-spin serve that could reach some eighty feet. The crowd would marvel and erupt in cheers.

Sinjin is the most relentless—and argumentative—competitor I've ever seen. If he doesn't agree with something in a match, be it the feel of a ball or a call, he will stand and contest it until he finally wins. He can also be very cagey and he utilized both of those traits in that match against the Brazilians.

For some reason the Brazilians believed that facing the sun took more energy out of you, so Bernard and his partner had been careful to choose the side of the court where their backs were to the sun. Conveniently, their rules also dictated that no side changes be made during a game. So, during the first game of the best two-out-of-three match, Bernard and his partner were using every stalling tactic in the book to keep their Yankee opponents facing the sun—in the hope that it would eventually melt them down. Bernard's partner would stop after every play to wipe himself off with a towel, seemingly just to stall for time. The first game alone lasted about an hour and a half, and the Brazilians won it.

The teams changed sides, and now it was Sinjin's turn. Tit for tat. Since they were serving him, he would slowly walk over to towel himself after every play. It drove Bernard and his partner crazy, which the fans recognized, and they began whistling and abusing Sinjin. No matter. Sinjin played it to the hilt, smilingly sauntering over to his towel, then back to serve, time after time. The jeering and whistling was ear-piercing, but Sinjin never relented. He and Randy won game two.

Interestingly, though Bernard wasn't getting many serves, he was the one who melted at 5–1 in the third game. Both his legs locked up in cramps and he was unable to move. Sinjin and Randy were in much better shape than those guys.

Although it wasn't part of the Triple Crown, we placed a lot of importance on the Pan-American Games in 1987. The event was in Indianapolis amd we wanted to show off our game to a national network audience. By then Chris Marlowe was building a career as a television broadcaster. At the Pan-Ams he did the coverage by himself—which he was able to do because he could talk so fast—and he was begging CBS to show more volleyball. It was unfortunate that they wouldn't, because there were some great matches and world-class teams competing, including Cuba and Argentina.

It was miserably hot and humid in Indianapolis, and I was still recovering from a broken hand—the result of a collision with Doug Partie in practice about a month before the tournament. Since it wasn't quite healed, the coaches were waiting until the important matches to use me.

In the semi-finals we met Argentina. They came out on fire and had us down 2–0 in games. Things weren't looking too good. Then an unusual event somehow got us on track. We were playing on an elevated court, about three feet above the normal arena floor. During the third game a blocked ball came off our blockers' hands and was headed out-of-bounds. Steve Timmons dove off the elevated floor, saved the ball, and crashed headfirst under the stands.

Although Jeff Stork set Steve's spectacular save to me, I was so freaked out that I hit it into the net. Immediately we sprinted to where Steve had disappeared.

"Steve, are you okay?" we shouted, peering down on a heap of flesh. Had he broken his neck? After several minutes he got to his feet, shook himself a little, then quietly sat on the bench for a few points before coming back into the game. That gave us the boost we needed, and we pulled it out 3–2. It also exemplified the level at which we were now competing. We had gotten to the point that we simply refused to be beaten by anyone—we were that confident.

That year had also brought some key personnel changes that still needed to be worked out. With the departures of Powers and Dvorak, Timmons was put in Powers's spot opposite the setter, and Doug Partie filled Steve's old middle blocking position. In the critical setting position, Stork had finally replaced Dvorak, who had gone back to Italy for good. Ctvrtlik, Partie, and Stork—who had replaced the '84 Olympic team starters—had by now paid their dues. They had learned how fiercely we practiced and how much pride we took in being the best team in the world.

Early on, some players on the team had questioned whether Ctvrtlik and Stork should be starters, particularly since they had both played for Marv Dunphy at Pepperdine. But they proved their critics wrong and turned out to be great players. Doug Partie also quickly filled his role as an exceptional sideout hitter and middle blocker.

The Cubans were always fun to play. Although they weren't quite on the same level as the Soviets, given their pure physical talent and volatile temperaments they were capable of beating any team in the world when they got hot. They'd come out for warm-ups, jump four feet off the ground, and bounce balls sixty feet in the air. Brute power. The fact that there was enmity between our governments seemed to heighten their high level of excitability even more when they played us.

In the finals, Cuba came out smoking. In fact, both teams were waiting for this showdown. We had faced them three times earlier that year and they had won twice. After the last match, which they won, they celebrated by sprinting around the arena in Havana, screaming and waving their jerseys in our faces. We didn't like that. And I was fired up for a shot at them in the Pan-Ams.

Rarely in my career—indoor or beach—did I have personal rivalries with any opponents, but one seemed to develop between Cuba's best player, Joel Despaigne, and me. Despaigne was an awesome player. He was so good that at times he carried the Cuban team by himself. There were games in which they'd set him in six rotations, the whole gym knowing where the ball was going, and he'd still put it away. Still, to have an offense so dependent on one guy is a dangerous way to live. On our team, a great part of our strength came from having many weapons: Timmons, Buck, Partie, Ctvrtlik, and me. With threats like those, teams weren't able to concentrate on stopping just one player.

Despaigne had only been on the team a few years in 1987, but when he came in as a nineteen-year-old he started on the wrong foot. Being so cocky, he liked to scream through the net after every spike. He tried that act with the Soviets too, but they largely didn't react. That stoic team didn't react to anything. They simply played and played well.

But when I saw Despaigne trying to diss the Soviets, I didn't like it. And when he started it against us, I liked it less. Unlike the Soviets, we would give it back to the Cubans, and we had some real scream-outs on the court. The emotional outbursts usually worked in our favor. If we were struggling against a team like Cuba or Brazil, that normally would prompt them to trash-talking across the net, giving us the wakeup call we needed. At that point, we'd proceed to dismantle them—both in the game and in the verbal jousting.

In Indianapolis the final against Cuba was a loud slugfest that went to the fifth game. The final point was particularly satisfying for me. On the last play of the game, they set the ball outside to Despaigne. I knew he would go for that incredibly sharp angle he loved to hit, so I came over and reached way inside. I got him. Point, game, match, Pan-American gold medal—and yelling rights.

CHAPTER TWELVE

SEOUL RELIEF

Though our team had reached the summit of the indoor game, I still wanted to join someone in dethroning Sinjin Smith and Randy Stoklos on the beach. One good opportunity was the second FIVB World Championships in Rio de Janeiro in 1988. Once again, Pat Powers and I were assigned to play in the extravaganza. Like the year before, the event was set up so one of our American teams would meet a Brazilian team in the finals. Pat and I knew we would have to beat Sinjin and Randy to get there.

We did. Pat got on a roll blocking and he wrought havoc on opponents. Powers was the best blocker I've ever seen on the beach. There are photos of him with his arms completely over the net and parallel to the ground. In soft sand that's not easy to do. Blocking like that intimidated hitters in Rio, so I was able to go behind and pick up their soft shots.

Pat was a great blocker, but he was not a great setter. I was having trouble hitting his sets since they were going all over the court. So I resorted to what I had learned at Santa Monica during my UCLA days. At State Beach in Santa Monica, what they called the "throw game" had developed, where you would jump and take the ball with two hands, guiding it to an open spot on the court. Without spiking, the throw game was half-serious but you learned ball placement. The Brazilians were using it a lot in Rio, as well as a one-hand dunk version of the spike. The FIVB rules were so lax then that almost any way of handling the ball was allowed. And the Brazilians were taking full advantage of it.

Besides, the Brazilians didn't usually play a power game. They took the serve with their hands, often shot the second ball over, and did not have to face the direction in which they set the ball. Their game was based more on deception than anything. And not pretty. We Americans thought the rules ridiculously loose, so I decided to fight fire with fire—and also handle Pat's drifting sets more effectively—by jumping and shooting the ball with two hands.

Crazy things happened in Rio. During the final, Pat and I found ourselves in a very long game against a Brazilian team that seemed amazingly prescient at finding the part of the court we chose to leave open. It was driving us crazy. They rarely hit the ball. It was like they had some kind of radar.

In a sense, they did. Two of their friends sitting in the stands, one at each end, were stealing our defensive signals every time we served. Before each play, whoever was blocking would signal the server by flashing one, two, or three fingers behind the back—indicating to what part of the court the defender should go. The two friends in the stands would read our signal, then hold up a painted sign with the corresponding number, relaying our defensive strategy to their buddies.

Halfway through the second game, Randy, who was watching in the stands, came down to give us some advice. Later we found out that the signal-stealers thought that Randy had discovered their ploy and was reporting it to us. The hilarious thing is that Randy hadn't seen anything, but that stopped them stealing our signals and we won that game and the match, 2–0. The next day in the paper there was a photo of one of the culprits, with a big grin, holding up a sign with a large "2" on it. Later it was one of the Brazilian players who told us what had gone on, and we had a good laugh together. After all, it was Rio.

The crowds can get hostile down there. In fact, the Brazilians are so fanatical about sports that their sports organizations paid some of their craziest fans to go to the Atlanta Olympics just to cheer. One of them, called Bola Sete, was a huge five-hundred-pound guy who was louder than any one hundred normal fans put together. And more colorful. In Brazil the noise never stops. But I love that. The louder it is, and the more it's against us, the better I like it.

As sports fans, the Brazilians and the Italians are in a class by themselves, although the Brazilians add more music and rhythm to their mayhem. It's a concerted effort, with everyone dancing and whistling at the same time. That whistling pierces your eardrums and can get so loud that you can't even hear someone on the court right next to you.

They can throw objects at you, spit on you from the balcony, and hurl all the worst kinds of verbal abuse. The funny thing is right after all that abuse they'll run up with a huge, friendly grin, begging, "Kiraly, please give me your shirt!"

In a preliminary match I got into a little bit of fan exchange myself. We were playing against Bernard Rajman, and I was waiting with great anticipation for his fabled sky ball. As the "journada de estrella" went up and up, I would kind of slouch and do a big yawn, patting my mouth in fake boredom, just before passing the ball. Perfectly. They whistled and hooted my irreverence wildly. I loved it.

We'd waited four years—since May 9, 1984, the day the Soviets announced the boycott—for the chance to play them in an Olympic finals. We still hadn't dethroned them in the big one. Also, we felt that the Seoul Olympics in 1988 was the optimal moment to expose our sport, especially to Americans.

In Seoul the media picked up on our story. They liked the image of our team—a lot of blond, tan, California-looking guys who displayed their emotion on the court. They particularly focused on the big, red-haired, flat-top of Steve Timmons. We were cool and hip in their eyes, and the volleyball world had long been talking about the emotion and cohesion of our team—"the American spirit." Maybe in part it was a reflection of our country's rise in world opinion and the demise of the Soviet empire. For so long, volleyball fans had watched the Soviets quietly mow down teams with nothing so much as a smile. We played the game with a vocal, wide-open, go-for-it style.

Getting to the finals was not an easy road. Steve was coming back from an injury and not quite fully recovered when we started the competition. Then, only ten days before the Games, Jeff Stork had seriously hurt his back. In the setting spot, Ricci Luyties started the competition.

We beat Japan, then the Netherlands, before coming up against a fiery Argentinean team—the same guys who had given us fits at the Pan-Ams the year before. They had some great players—Raul Quiroga, Hugo Conte, and Waldo Cantor. Quiroga and Conte were streak hitters, and in the first two and a half games they were devastating. In fact, we were close to losing the match 3–0 when Dunphy put in Stork to serve. Stork delivered a couple of bullets, which got us a few needed points and back on track. We pulled out the game. The fourth game was touch-and-go as well, until we clawed to a 17–15 win. By the fifth we had gained the momentum and smoked them 15–8. It was our only real scare of the tournament.

In the semis we faced Brazil and things got pretty hot on the court. We were hammering them when a couple of their young guys started scream-ing through the net at us. Wrong thing to do. We pelted them after that. Right after the last point, one of their young bucks was jawing at Tim-mons who was standing behind me. I mistakenly thought the Brazilian was directing his taunting at me, so I went nuts and retaliated. Television closed in on my contorted face. For a long time after that, people asked me what it was that I was screaming at my opponent. I just told them we were scheduling a time to exchange Christmas presents.

Interestingly, I don't remember too much about the gold-medal match against the Soviets. I do remember that it was 13–13 in the first game, and I had a chance to score the fourteenth point. I got roofed. We lost the game and I was kicking myself for that error. In the second and third games we came back with strong wins and were cruising in the fourth, until we hit a lull. I missed a few passes and we uncharacteristically gave up some easy points.

Suddenly it was like the wind had stopped and our boat was stalled. What we did then was to take some big risks in a couple of plays. I remember that their great left-hander, Yuri Antonov, was slicing our block apart all match. I was one-on-one with him and decided to spread my arms really wide with a V-block, thinking he would hit a sharp angle. It was poor blocking form, and a fluke, but one of my hands smothered his attack for the block. It got me going again, we got a few more stuffs, and quickly we were up 12–7. At that point we couldn't be denied.

The thirteenth point was memorable for me because it typified how we had played during those five or six years when we were the best team in the world. One of their big hitters cranked a cross-court shot and I dug it. Stork set it to Steve and he drilled it, without it even being touched. That was our style. We weren't a dominant blocking team, but we were a team that kept the ball alive until Timmons would finish the play with a bomb.

Eric Sato, who was only five-foot-eleven but had a bullet jump serve, had done a phenomenal job of subbing-in during the tournament and getting us points. In fact, I think he ended half of our matches in Seoul with aces. Dunphy put him in when we had match point, and he fired a serve that was mispassed over the net to Scott Fortune. Fortune blasted it straight down for the fifteenth point.

The next thing I knew, we were celebrating. Steve jumped off the referee's stand just like he did in Los Angeles in 1984. But for me, this one was a different feeling—an overwhelming sense of relief mixed with accomplishment. I had stressed so hard for those two weeks in Seoul that now I was entirely spent. I didn't have enough energy to go to the closing ceremonies. I had nothing left. I got together with Janna and our family at a sponsor reception and we kicked back with a couple of big Cokes. No big celebration like in 1984. I was simply too exhausted.

After our second gold medal, it was natural for people to ask which was the better team—'84 or '88? My answer is still the same: It's too hard for me to compare the two. Both were great teams. The big difference was that the '84 team never got a chance to play against the world's best because of the boycott. It's a comparison best left alone.

More importantly, we had matched a Soviet record by winning two Olympics in a row, and won a legitimate Triple Crown. I felt that winning two Olympics back-to-back was the greatest thing we'd done. Winning is one thing; staying on top after winning is another. It's much harder. So many Olympians have had just one great performance. Mark Spitz won seven golds in the Munich Olympics, which was a phenomenal accomplishment, but I admire longevity much more—in Carl Lewis, for instance, who did it over four Olympics. Had it not been for the '80 boycott, he probably would have won medals in five Olympics. That's unbelievable. The pressure you face as a favorite, including the pressure you put on yourself, is the ultimate test for an athlete. And the one of which I'm most proud.

My contract with the USA Men's Team ran through September of 1989. Italy was making attractive overtures to all the starters on the 1988 team and a few, like Jeff Stork and Bob Ctvrtlik, left for the big lire. I was committed to the USA Team but, more importantly, I was itching to play on the beach full-time. No Italy for me.

Looking toward the 1989 beach season I talked with Mike Dodd about hooking up, but he was still committed to Hov. Dodd mentioned that one of the young lions from Marine Street in Manhattan Beach, Brent Frohoff, had been playing really well. So I checked him out. I gave him a call and we started a partnership by winning our first tournament, crushing the top team, Sinjin and Randy, 15–2. We had pretty good success, winning four events in what was another half-season for me.

One thing I tried again in 1989 was the *Superstars* event in Miami, since I was invited back. This time the format was a little different, in that basketball was an event we all had to do. I'd never played much basketball, and when I did I was horrible. We were required to shoot three-point shots. A lot of mouths dropped when they saw me setting the ball rather than shooting it from some thirty feet away. I even made a couple, but that event didn't get me any points. Still, I finished fourth overall and, I hope, upheld the reputation of volleyball players everywhere.

For the first time in my life, indoor volleyball had left me stale. I still had some USA Team commitments, mostly tours, but I was totally flat. I had nothing left to give, no motivation at all. Knowing there was no serious competition to look forward to, I was just going through the motions—burnt out. And I couldn't take being away from Janna two hundred days out of a year anymore. I decided to retire from the indoor sport.

I talked to Steve about it and he decided to quit as well. We played our last match in the Los Angeles Forum in front of about twelve thousand people—against the Soviet Union, which was a nice way to finish. We won, 3–0, which was even nicer. I wasn't overwhelmed with emotion that night. I had given so much to the USA Team that everything had already been left on the court.

I was ready to move on. I was only twenty-eight and excited to get back to the beach. It had been a long time—I hadn't played a full beach season since 1976 when I was fifteen. The Italians were still calling, and the more I ignored them the higher the offers got. But I'd had enough of gyms for a while. Sinjin Smith was chalking up more tournament wins every year. It was time to get back on the sand.

CHAPTER THIRTEEN

ITALIAN WINTERS, CALIFORNIA SUMMERS

I have never felt more useless than I did on the evening that our first son, Kristian, was born. It was September 21, 1990. I had taken Janna to the hospital about midday. At six or seven o'clock her labor got really intense, but there was absolutely nothing I could do to help.

The doctor's plan was to give her an epidural—a shot that would numb her from the waist down. But her cervix dilated so fast that it was too late to give her the shot. During those twenty-five minutes her pain seemed unbearable.

"Rub my back!" she'd plead. "No, stop!" she'd tell me a few moments later. Nothing gave her any relief. Finally, they took her into the labor room.

I followed with a video camera, taping some of the experience until right before the birth. By then the doctor had put up a screen at her waist. He stood behind it and explained everything as he delivered Kristian. I stayed next to Janna's face.

Kristian came out screaming. I got the honor of cutting the umbilical cord, then they cleaned him up and took him to get weighed. About midnight, he was brought to Janna for her to breast-feed him for the first time. I stood dumbstruck, totally amazed to have a child—to see my wife as a mother.

I was excited but I was in shock too. I tried without success to sleep next to Janna on an extra gurney. About three o'clock in the morning I went home. Utterly exhausted, I slept through the alarm.

"Oh, my god!" I leaped out of bed as soon as my eyes opened and I saw the clock. It was about 10:00 o'clock—late on my first day as a dad.

I jumped up and drove to the hospital, berating myself all the way. Worse, that same night I was committed to play in the Team Cup, a six-man exhibition series, in the Los Angeles Forum where the Lakers and the Kings played. Should I play or not?

I was torn. I felt an obligation to Steve Timmons's wife, Jeannie, who managed Forum tennis and volleyball events and organized the series. I called her and she assured me not to worry about missing the match. Still, my sense of commitment—or habit perhaps—got the best of me and I decided to play. On the court my mind was completely elsewhere. My second screw-up in one day.

For the first three days after Kristian's birth I went around in a dream-like state. With an infant, the mother is so crucial but the father is superfluous. I wanted to give my new son some attention but he didn't need anything from me. It was a feeling of uselessness and confusion.

I found out later that that's normal for new dads. And after we spent some time in Italy, I also learned I wasn't doing as bad a job as I'd first thought. One day an Italian teammate who had a two-year-old daughter asked me, "Karch, do you ever change Kristian's diapers?"

"Of course. Every day," I replied.

He was floored. The guy had changed his daughter's diapers only twice in her entire life!

After three days we brought Kristian home, and once Janna walked through the door with him, our house was never the same. We were now a family. I was fixated on Kristian, constantly taking videos of him—sleeping, awake, feeding. But it wouldn't last as long as I hoped. I'd have to leave soon. Months earlier, Janna and I had decided to go to Italy, although with misgivings. We had felt great ambivalence about going to a foreign country, knowing that Kristian would be so young and that we would be brand-new, first-time parents far from family, friends, and our pediatrician. But they had offered a lot of money and we felt that we could set ourselves financially by going.

That year turned out to be by far the hardest in Janna's life and one of the hardest in mine. About two weeks after Kristian's birth, Steve Timmons and I flew to Italy. In the Italian pro league two foreign players were allowed to play on each club team, and it was arranged that Steve and I would play on the same team—teammates again and that was a great feeling. The volleyball officials of our new club, Il Messaggero, picked us up at the airport in Milan. They had a new Fiat car for each of us to drive to our apartments in Ravenna, about three hours away and situated on the Adriatic Sea.

I didn't know what to bring, especially with the new baby, so I played it safe and brought too much. Boxes and boxes. The Italians were stupefied at all the stuff, which barely fit into the two cars.

They dropped us off that night at our apartments in Marina di Ravenna, the neighboring seaport town of Ravenna. Aldis Berzins, who had played in Ravenna before, suggested that we live near the beach. However, we didn't know that while Marina di Ravenna is a resort town in the summer, it's completely dead in the winter.

There was a phone and I called Janna immediately. "Hey, it's okay! We've got a nice two-bedroom apartment. Washer and dryer. And we're right by a park."

For me it was cool. I'd been on the USA Men's Team for so many years, stayed in so many dives in so many places, that I could handle anything. Even today, all I need is a decent bed and I'm fine.

When Janna walked in the door about a week later, she almost fell over. To her, this was an old, dark, dingy apartment. To top it off, the wood floors were infested with fleas—to which she's like a magnet—and she woke up her first morning with about fifty bites. Steve's and his wife's reactions were identical to mine and Janna's. Steve thought the place was fine. When Jeannie arrived she thought it was a dump.

The next morning the team managers, the *dirigenti,* showed us around Ravenna—population about one hundred thousand. The city is beautiful— over a thousand years old with an art history that dates all the way back to the Byzantine Empire. Like most old Italian cities, the center is a labyrinth of little streets built before cars existed. Of course, it had some great restaurants and we were given discounts at several. One was in the Hotel Romeo where we went the first day for lunch.

The setter of the team, Fabio Vullo, was an exceptionally nice guy who spoke pretty good English, so he accompanied us. Only minutes after diving into our first pasta, an older, diminutive man walked up to our table. He introduced himself as Pierbruno, and plopped himself down, talking and gesturing animatedly. His English was impeccable.

"I'm sorry for my English," he said. We sat there, even Fabio, wondering Who is this guy? It turned out that he loved Americans and had befriended a lot of American athletes, as well as American jazz musicians, who had come to Ravenna. The fact that he had tracked us down within hours of our arrival blew us away.

Pierbruno became a good friend. He was a gentleman farmer, married, but he still loved to flirt with women. To us he seemed the consummate Italian. We had some unforgettable meals at his two-hundred-year-old farmhouse. All the produce was grown on his farm. If it was a special occasion Pierbruno would exclaim, "I will kill a pig! And make sausage myself!"

The pasta was always handmade and Pierbruno's best friend, Germano, who had spent two years as a POW in Texas during World War II, would prepare it in gargantuan pans over a wood stove. The wine was also made with Pierbruno's own grapes and poured out of the cask into any old bottle. I'm not a wine aficionado, but that wine tasted as good as any I've ever had. At moments, Steve and I would sit back after a fabulous meal, sipping that wine, and realize what an incredible experience eating can be.

We started practicing right away, and after two practices Steve and I had to ask each other, "What in the world is going on here?" We were used to a very high level of intensity on the national team. We also knew that this was the premier league in the world, with most of the world's best players competing. Each team was allowed two foreigners, so it was effectively a world all-star league. It seemed logical to us that the practices would come close to the same organization and intensity that we had on the USA Men's Team. But this wasn't even close.

Steve and I were each getting about $500,000 that first year so we felt obligated to perform extremely well. We weren't there for a paid vacation. In turn, there were very high expectations of us.

The old adage "you play like you practice" is true. Not only did Steve and I want to play well, but we also wanted to be challenged. We wanted the Italians to be challenged too. Our coach, Daniele Ricci, knew his volleyball reasonably well but he was far too sweet a guy. He asked nothing of us in practice. Steve and I immediately set out to coax him to design certain practices as well as to be more demanding of us—not just for the starters, but for the second six players as well. In Italy the second team usually accepted their roles as non-starters, so they were unmotivated in practice. "Why try? We aren't gonna play anyway."

By contrast, on the USA Men's Team if any player ever let a ball fall to the ground with no one going after it—first *or* second team—all hell broke loose. The coaches stopped the practice and punished the guilty player with excruciating drills. In those first few days in Italy, balls were dropping all the time with guys not even taking a step toward them. Steve and I were astounded. By the third or fourth day, when a ball dropped we were screaming, yelling, and kicking the balls. The Italian guys thought we were nuts.

In the end, players got a little better in practice but we never really got through to the coach, particularly not about making the second-team guys work harder. Their habits were too ingrained. I was surprised to learn later that several of those second-team players are now on the Italian national team.

During the two years we were there, the Italian league was in its heyday and salaries reached all-time highs. Our owner was Raul Gardini, arguably the richest man in Italy. One of his properties was *Il Messaggero,* a large daily newspaper in Italy, which is why our team was named Il Messaggero Ravenna. Other team owners included Sylvio Berlusconi—the Ted Turner of Italy, who later became prime minister—and the Benetton family of apparel fame. At that time it was in vogue for all these wealthy people to have sports teams, and bidding wars for world-class players was a result of their capricious acquisitiveness.

We had a talented team. Fabio Vullo could have easily been the Italian national team's starting setter, but he'd had a few bad experiences with the coaches and so he only played in the league. He was six-foot-five and could hit with either hand. Andrea Gardini, six-foot-nine, was a middle hitter who worked astonishingly well with Vullo. Roberto Masciarelli was our other quick hitter, a nice and funny guy, and a good player too.

About a week after his arrival in Italy, Kristian came down with a severe case of colic. From early October until mid-January, he was either sleeping, eating, or screaming—mostly screaming, in perpetual agony. If we put our ears on his stomach, we could hear gas bubbles constantly coursing through his system. A new baby screaming most of the night makes for a trying existence. I felt so bad for him and Janna, and it affected my play.

Kristian's and Janna's tribulations were made worse by cultural differences. Our USA Men's Team gave us freedom when we were off the court. However, the Italians liked to control every part of a player's day. Even for home games we'd have to get up early, go to a practice, then go to a two-and-a-half-hour lunch. By the time we were done it was midafternoon—time to go home, then leave an hour later for the gym to tape up and have meetings for the match. After the match there was a mandatory dinner for the team.

It was worse for away games. A Sunday-afternoon game meant leaving early Saturday morning—to allow practice time on the opponent's court—and getting back late Sunday night or Monday morning. So sometimes Janna was stuck for forty-eight hours with Kristian. I still don't know how she did it. She was utterly deprived of sleep. Afterward, she told me she would have gone home except for two reasons: She wanted me to have a chance to bond with Kristian, and she was terrified of taking him on the plane all that way in that condition. Imagine having the seat next to him!

We had Mondays off and that was about the only day Janna could get out of the house alone. One Monday morning I had some reggae music on and was holding my screaming son. I started dancing to the music and suddenly he got quiet. Janna returned about three hours later to find me drenched with sweat, still dancing. Every time I stopped, Kristian would start crying again. But at least something worked. I discovered that by holding him across my stomach and bouncing and jiggling him, it provided him some relief. We constantly danced with him from then on. But for those first three and a half months, life had been really tough for Janna and him.

Not surprisingly, I didn't play well during the first couple of months. I felt frustrated at not having enough time to help Kristian and Janna, felt like I wasn't able to be a good enough dad or husband, and felt guilty during much of the time that the team needed me to be elsewhere. The newspapers were criticizing me with statements like, "Karch is just here for the money and a vacation," or "He's not the player we thought he was."

I learned during those few months that it was best not to read the papers. Everything gets so blown out of proportion—both the good and the bad. Thank God they didn't have sports talk radio like we do here. I would have been ripped to shreds.

Pressure was building within our club's management as well. Although we were winning, the first part of our season was against the weaker teams. We weren't impressive—I surely wasn't—and it started coming to a head.

For a particularly important home match, management had the team stay in a hotel in Marina di Ravenna. They felt that we needed to be away from our wives. Their belief was that sleeping with your loved one would sap your energy. Well, after dinner Steve and I decided to walk to our own apartments since we only lived three blocks away and preferred to sleep in our own beds. When the *dirigenti* got wind of it, they flipped out. I had to apologize to the coach and the management. Soon after, I missed a team breakfast in order to help Janna with Kristian who was having a terrible morning. They went nuts again.

I was trying to be a better dad and a good player, and it was a hard act to balance. The finale came when we played against a Brazilian team in the World Club Championship, which was a four-day competition between the world's best club teams. I had a pulled calf muscle and didn't start, but to the public it looked as though my recent poor play had gotten me benched. That was the low point. I came in after the first game, but we lost the match. It was considered a disaster and a wakeup call. I must have sensed it because my play suddenly started to kick in.

Our team got on a roll. In our twenty-six game regular season we set a new league record by winning the first twenty-five. In our final match we dropped the fifth game, 15–13, against Mediolanum Milano. That was as close as you can get to a perfect season.

Especially satisfying about that performance was dispelling the Italian myth that you can't win on the road. Over there it was a foregone conclusion: Play away and you lose. Steve and I helped to change that mentality, at least on our team. I always believed that playing in front of your home crowd put more pressure on you than on the visitors. I loved playing away, especially in front of big crowds. The best part was to silence those crowds by walking away with a win.

The team managers kept asking us to move closer to town, but we didn't want to put them out with all the time and trouble of moving us. Finally, as Marina di Ravenna became even more quiet in the dead of winter, we agreed to move. When you win in Italy, you're treated like a king. In January of 1991, we saw what royal treatment could be, when we were given a three-level house in the center of Ravenna. It was like a palace. Marble floors, satellite TV with English and American channels, expensive furniture of our choice, even an installed garbage disposal in the kitchen—something most Italians had never seen. The space was ample enough that both families could live there comfortably.

Living in Ravenna was much nicer than being isolated outside it. When the weather warmed, we enjoyed bicycling and visiting the famous Byzantine churches with their priceless mosaic ceilings. More importantly, Kristian was over his colic. What a godsend that was! We could actually take him places now. Predictably, my play improved as well.

"Ciao, Karch! Ciao, Kristian!" Riding our bikes around town, everywhere we went people talked to us. I would ride with Kristian on my bike and the Italians loved to make a fuss over him. Ravenna had never won a national championship, and as the playoffs approached the town became galvanized.

The national championship is called Lo Scudetto and it is decided by a series of playoffs, not too different from the NBA basketball playoffs. After the eliminating rounds were finished, the championship came down to a three-out-of-five series against Maxicono Parma—the team Jeff Stork had played on. We won the first match 3–0 at home, and the second 3–0 in Parma. That set up the third match in Ravenna. If we won it, the title would be ours.

The town was buzzing with excitement when that Saturday came around. People were fighting for tickets. The dome-shaped arena was absolutely brimming with people by game time. When we ran out on the floor I was almost blown down by the loudest noise I'd ever heard in my life. Before the game, freon airhorns had been passed out to everyone and six thousand of them went off at the same time. I had to cover my ears, the sound was so painful.

With that kind of crazed enthusiasm we couldn't have lost. In fact, we ripped them 3–0 and the town erupted in joy. After the match, while relaxing at home, we were startled by a boisterous commotion in the front yard. We looked outside, and right before us a parade was filing past our house. The fans were singing songs they had made up about our team and its two Americans. Something to the effect of "We are the only team that has Kiraly and Timmons, and we're the best."

Steve and I came out on the balcony waving the team flag and they screamed for us to come down. We joined them, signed autographs, gave away T-shirts, and took photos. It was an incredible feeling of appreciation—the only times I've felt that in this country were after winning the Olympics.

Despite the hoopla, we were anxious to get back home. But there were more requisite celebrations and the Italians definitely know how to celebrate. The next day, Sunday, we called some guys from the team and invited them out to the beach to play a little beach volleyball, just for fun. Apparently they told a few friends, because the word got out and over a thousand people showed up to watch us knock the ball around in the sand.

That evening we had the big team banquet where everyone gave speeches. When it was my turn I told them, in Italian, "When you lose there are always questions. When you win there are none. Next year there will be no questions." Not profound, not eloquent, but they loved it nonetheless.

It was a memorable night at the seafood restaurant—especially the food poisoning I got. That wouldn't have been so bad were we not scheduled to drive to Milan early the next morning and then fly home. I kept throwing up but I was going home no matter what. So I told our driver to keep going, and I lost it out the window at seventy miles an hour.

How ecstatic we were when we finally got home! At five o'clock the next morning, jet-lagged to the gills, Janna and I took Kristian to Ralph's supermarket. "Oh, my god!" we marveled. The limitless selection of food, the wide aisles with no little old ladies running us down, and it's open twenty-four hours.

And there were other forgotten pleasures. I could indulge myself again with my favorite cuisine, Mexican, at any number of good restaurants. We could rent our favorite movies and watch them again in the comfort of our own home. *The Sting, Butch Cassidy and the Sundance Kid, It's a Wonderful Life*—my all-time choices were here just for the asking. We had learned that the best way to appreciate how fortunate we are in America is to live elsewhere for a while. Then we could appreciate such simple pleasures as sitting on our plush carpet.

One of the few things I did in Italy, ouside of playing volleyball, was to write a diary—a series of articles about my experiences—for *Volleyball Monthly*. I haven't read them since, but if I did I'm sure I would see them as extremely whiny and complaining. Perhaps they were overly harsh, but it was a very hard year for us. Being parents for the first time, with a colicky baby in a foreign country, was no fun. Janna was so completely occupied with a constantly crying child that she didn't even have time to learn the language. Even with the amount of money we got, we still weren't convinced it was worth going back for a second year. Sitting on our soft carpet felt awfully nice.

One thing about Kent Steffes, my beach partner in the 1996 Olympics, is that he doesn't lack confidence. After the 1989 beach season, we met for lunch to discuss a possible partnership. I asked him, "How do you think we could do next season?"

"I think we can win seventeen of the twenty-two events," he answered.

I slid my chair back a little and peered at him. No team had ever won that many in a season. Considering that we had never played together, and that Sinjin and Randy were still the best team, his reply seemed a bold statement to say the least. Overconfident, in fact. Yet, somehow I liked his big thinking. I certainly didn't think we could win seventeen out of twenty-two but his prediction that day actually turned out to be right on track—it would just take a few years.

Leaving the restaurant, I had to decide whether I was going to go with this brash twenty-one-year-old or stay with Brent Frohoff. One thing that struck me about Kent was that he looked really serious in his training. He was physically stronger than Brent, although he wasn't quite as gifted in some areas—for example, Frohoff had a great pair of hands for setting. But Brent sometimes seemed to wear down in tournaments. I wasn't sure if it was a lack of training or if he just wasn't that powerful by constitution, but it was common knowledge that Kent was one of the best-trained players on the tour.

I decided to give Kent a try. In the 1990 season we went out and won an early event, but then we quickly hit a lull. We only won one of the next nine. Since Kent was the less experienced player, teams went after him with most of the serves. He wasn't wearing down but he hadn't yet become the sideout machine he would later be. Plus, I wasn't having as much fun playing with him—we didn't seem to really enjoy being together on the court. Our chemistry just wasn't very good.

In our quest to dethrone Smith and Stoklos, we had won only three times in the twelve matches in which we faced them. Finally I got impatient with the results and decided to go back with Brent. I handled the breakup miserably. After contemplating the change, I told Brent that I was going back with him, and he immediately went to tell his current partner, Scott Ayakatubby. Ayakatubby, in turn, called Kent right away—before I'd had a chance to call him. Hearing it from a second source upset him. Understandably so.

In beach volleyball we have what we call "karma matches" and it was inevitable that I would encounter one during my career. This is when a guy who got dumped by his partner later gets a chance to play against him.

Vengeance would be a mild description. A karma match is one that the whole tour is suddenly interested in watching. In my second tournament with Frohoff in San Jose, we ran into Kent. He was frothing to beat me and he did. He and Dan Vrebalovich took us down in a double finals.

Later I heard Kent say that it was a good thing for him that I dropped him; maybe he had become a little complacent—gotten to the top too quickly—and needed some motivation. I sure gave him that (though I didn't mean to) in the form of a personal vendetta, if nothing else. Afterward he stepped up his game a notch.

As for Brent and me, we recovered to win five of the twelve remaining events. It was after this 1990 season that I had my moved my family to Italy. The eight months there were such a grind that I'd needed some time off when we returned in June of 1991. By the time I was ready to hit the sand, half the season had already passed.

As usual, I was wondering who to play with. Kent had started that '91 season with Tim Hovland but he called me when I got home. Ironically, Hov also called me to ask about playing together—unbeknownst to each other. Typically, Kent felt very positive about our chances to dominate the tour. Even though I had handled our breakup poorly the year before, he wanted to pair up again—a resolute gesture that surprised me.

"I think you ought to play with Kent. The guy's really improved. He's gotten very steady and his mental toughness is there," was how Chris Marlowe evaluated Steffes when I sought his advice. My dad, and some other people, had the same impression. I went with Kent.

Our first tournament was in Cape Cod and our second start together was inauspicious—a fifth. We got knocked out of the winner's bracket on Saturday night, which was a blow. On Sunday morning at breakfast Kent seemed kind of quiet and down. I thought I knew why.

"Kent," I told him, "it looks to me like you're playing tentatively. I don't want you to think that you have to play perfectly or I'll change partners next weekend. I was too quick to break up our partnership last year, and I want you to know that I'm committed to our partnership for a long time. We just need to settle down and play without any worries."

As it turned out, we didn't play very well that day either. Pat Powers and Adam Johnson knocked us out of the tournament, but maybe my words of support bore fruit. We won the next four tournaments in a row.

Smith and Stoklos had been the best team on the tour for the past five years. Kent and I won six out of the last nine tournaments in 1991, while Sinjin and Randy won only one event. They were clearly no longer the best team—Kent and I were. It looked like I'd found the partner I needed, not only for now, but for a long time.

Time had assuaged our bad memories of Italy, and had eliminated Kristian's colic as well. Janna and I decided to return. It was much easier the second time around. My sister Kati came over for several months to help with Kristian, and that gave Janna some free time to travel a little. Unfortunately, I didn't have the time to go with her.

Italy can be an incredibly romantic place and I regret that Janna and I never had the chance to enjoy a season there, just the two of us, to be able to go to Venice, Florence, Rome—sightsee, eat great food, visit museums. It didn't, it couldn't, happen with a one-year-old.

Happily, our second season was shorter than normal because of the approaching Barcelona Olympics. The season would end, at the latest, the first week of April 1992. By virtue of our having been the Italian champions the year before, we were entered in both the World and European Club Championships—prestigious competitions that meant a lot to our club and to the city as well.

In the finals of the European Club championship, we played against a strong club team from Athens on their home floor, in front of twenty-three-thousand people. The night before the match, Steve Timmons and I were out strolling. All the food scents in the air got to me and I decided to buy a gyro sandwich from a street vendor. Bad idea. After I ridded my stomach all night, I couldn't get out of bed the next morning. Steve tried to fire me up by saying, "Come on, Karch! This is worth $50,000!" That was how much our bonus would be for winning.

By game time I was able to move around enough to help the team. We played a great match and blew them away. Steve was phenomenal, as always. In the course of our whole two years there, he was unstoppable. The whole gym would know that the set was going to Steve, but he would terminate the play with a kill. He and the setter, Fabio Vullo, really clicked. Fabio learned to hang the set far in front of the ten-foot line so Steve could broad-jump out of the back row and bang it, landing at the net.

After the match in Athens it was strange to be on the victory stand and hear the Italian anthem being played rather than "The Star Spangled Banner." I could barely hear it. The Greek fans whistled the entire time, still furious about losing. As soon as the anthem finished, they started firing coins at us, actually giving some of our guys skull cuts. We hid in the locker room and waited for over an hour before venturing out to the bus.

They take it really seriously over there. Those are the kinds of matches I always wished that sports media people in this country could witness— that unique combination of athletic ability and passion, and the intensity of the fans. Unfortunately, the powerful people in American sports haven't witnessed that show as yet. Maybe one day.

The regular season didn't go as well. We earned the third seed in the playoffs with a 22–4 record. Not bad, but not like the year before. Still, we made it to the finals of the playoffs. And we won both the World Club and European Club championships, which were huge accomplishments.

But I thought the most dramatic event that year was the contractions Janna started having in the middle of January. She was then six and a half months pregnant and suddenly she had to stay in bed, essentially immobile. The contractions soon became stronger and her doctor decided that she had to come home. In early February I brought Janna and Kristian back to California.

One of my worst mornings ever was two days later when I had to wave good-bye to them. I had to go back to Italy alone, for two more months. I was crushed. As Kristian grew older, I was feeling more useful as a dad— in fact, I loved being a father more every day.

During the semi-finals of the playoffs, I saw that there were six possible scenarios I could be faced with. In three of them I would go home for good—if we lost. If we won three matches to zero, or three to one, I'd have time before the final round began to go home for a few days while the doctor induced Janna's labor. Consequently, I had five out of six chances of being present when Janna gave birth. Of course, the sixth scenario is what happened: We won three matches to two, 17–15 in the final game of the final match—and I wouldn't be there for the birth of our second child. Making that phone call to Janna was incredibly difficult. We were both terribly disappointed.

"Okay, Karch. I'm going to go outside, do some jumping jacks, and have this baby! I'm not holding it in any longer." My wife had had enough. She went into labor as the first match of the final round was about to start. All I could think about was missing the birth of our second child. I played horribly and we lost the match 3–0. I called right afterward and Janna was already in the delivery room. They told me to call back in twenty minutes.

Kory was born a minute before my next call to the hospital—from a cell phone on the team bus—and I screamed to the guys, "Sono un babbo di nuovo!" Which means, I'm a dad again.

We proceeded to lose the next two matches 3–0, 3–0, with Parma thoroughly dominating us as much as we had dominated them in the final round the year before. It was a poor note on which to end our time in Italy, but many of the fans still came out to the gym one more time to beg us to return for another year. Steve and I were touched.

He and I had each earned close to a million dollars that second year in Italy. Soon after, the Italian economy fell and the salaries of pro athletes plummeted with it. Still, teams from Italy called for several more years trying to lure me back, but my priorities had changed.

Barcelona was around the corner and I had only a few days after I touched down in L.A. to decide whether I was going to play in the Olympics. The new head coach, Fred Sturm, had earlier paid me a visit in Italy to discuss my plans. I stayed uncommitted. Now it was imperative that I attend practices in San Diego right away if I wanted to play.

Although I knew that most of the guys from the '88 Olympic Team were coming back, I had to ask myself, "Do I really want to go back into the gym six days from now?"

My answer was no. I'd been in Italy, away from Janna, and Kory had just been born. I was not one of the twelve most-motivated indoor players in the country. That would be unfair to those guys—wasting everyone's time if I was not trying my hardest.

Of course, there was considerable media hype about making Olympic volleyball history by capturing a third gold medal in a row, but in my own mind I wasn't certain we could win again. I had been impressed with the Italian players we'd seen in Italy. I also felt that Steve's and my skills weren't quite what they had been a year earlier.

The USA Team went on to win a bronze in Barcelona, gaining world-wide attention by shaving their heads in protest of an off-court committee decision that gave Japan a controversial victory in the first match. That event seemed to cast a pall over the whole experience, and I must say I was happy not to have become the ugliest Olympic player in history with a newly bald head. In retrospect, I think we might have won it had I played. Did I feel guilty? No. The USVBA had had three years to replace me since my retirement. In the end, I didn't have it in my heart to go back into another gym.

One unfortunate result of my decision not to play in Barcelona was the impact it had on my friendship with Steve. He and I hadn't talked much about Barcelona when we were in Italy earlier that year. However, as soon as I got home Chris Marlowe had called to find out what I was going to do. Beach or Barcelona? I said beach and he announced it on national television that weekend during an AVP event. I called Steve shortly afterward to inform him of my decision but the word was already out. He may have been upset about not hearing it from me first.

I mishandled the affair. Part of me didn't want to be a bearer of bad news, but I should have told him first. Suddenly there was a distance between us. Actually, we had grown apart a little the summer before, simply because we were leading different lives now. Janna and I had become parents and, after returning from the first season in Italy, we just wanted to spend most of our time at home with Kristian. More so when Kory came. Steve had started a clothing company, Redsand, and he was busy with that. Also he and Jeannie were much more socially active in California. In time they would go through a divorce.

I called Steve right before the Olympics to wish him good luck and tell him that I hoped they'd bring back the gold medal. Afterward, every six months or so, I'd call and leave a message. Steve is a great guy—the best guy I ever played with and the most fun guy I ever played with. Maybe we'll spend time together again one day. We went to his wedding last year. He and his wife, Debbie, recently came by with their new daughter, Spencer. He seemed very happy. He always wanted a family and now he has one. His apparel company continues to do well. I'm really happy for him. We shared many special times together.

I was very content to stay on the beach in 1992. After so many unfulfilled and frustrating years, I got back to where I wanted to be—one half of the best team on the beach. Kent Steffes had matured into a phenomenal player and we won sixteen out of the nineteen AVP tournaments that year, including thirteen in a row. I know that achievement will be extremely difficult to match. The talent pool on the AVP Tour has gotten stronger and deeper, and will only continue to do so.

As the summer ended, things looked good. Janna and I were ecstatic to be able to stay close to home with our two boys. I was gone on weekends only during the summer and I could manage my own workout schedule during the rest of the year—close to home. I knew that I'd never play in shoes again. I'd end my career where I started. On the beach.

CHAPTER FOURTEEN

THE GOLDEN ERA

It looks like Sinjin and Randy have to leave the country to win a tournament," I said.

It was at a Hermosa Beach tournament in 1992 that I made that statement to a reporter. It caused a stir, but it illustrated the heightening frustration and ill feeling between the AVP and the FIVB. Obviously, it also reflected my assessment of the level of play of those two guys.

As the AVP sailed into its strongest era—prize money in 1993 and 1994 was about $4,000,000 and NBC aired sixteen live broadcasts of the tour in 1994—the tussle for control of the sport of world beach volleyball was getting into full swing. The game was booming here, but loud rumbles were being heard outside the country as well. FIVB president Ruben Acosta had been on a mission to develop and control the sport since he took office in 1984, and he was making good headway.

Typically he went about it in autocratic fashion, using all the clout available to him. That was a lot. He had infiltrated the Brazilian scene and had gotten the hugely successful Rio event adopted as the annual FIVB World Beach Volleyball Championships. He had also begun to nurture the sport in Europe and Asia, even though beach volleyball doubles had scant history there. Still, he had tremendous financial resources, the green light from national volleyball federations in almost two hundred countries, and the support of the International Olympic

Committee—including a close association with IOC president Juan Antonio Samaranch.

In this country he had the automatic blessing of the USVBA, but that historically weak organization didn't count for much. Certainly not in beach volleyball. He knew that the game was developed by the best players—members of the AVP who had led the charge to make it a legitimate sport. The lines between the AVP and the FIVB were quickly drawn. If Acosta wanted to establish a beachhead in the United States, he needed an ally here—someone who knew the sport, and the AVP, inside and out. He couldn't have found a better one than Sinjin Smith.

Sinjin has done as much for beach volleyball as any player in its history. He was a tireless promoter in the early days of the AVP, freely giving his time to show up at promotions and graciously signing endless autographs. He's proven his care for the sport. He's also ambitious and will relentlessly fight for what he wants, on the court and in the political arena. That same hot pursuit of his agenda would come to alienate him from the AVP players and me—an ongoing conflict that would have an interesting conclusion at the Atlanta Olympics.

Sinjin's mentor was Ron Von Hagen and that was a very good fit for Sinjin's style of play. Von Hagen played in an era when there was no clock, which meant the main goal was to never give up a point. Whether it took twenty minutes or three days, you sided out until you won the game. Von Hagen was the best prepared on the beach physically for that type of game, and his ability to stay focused until the final point was also legendary.

Sinjin became that same kind of player. I also think that he provided the mental toughness and consistency in his great partnership with Stoklos, and that helped bring Randy's game up a notch. Sinjin took more serves than any player in history, and put more balls away. The rest of us stood to learn from that.

I also learned a lot about competition from Sinjin. We were both setter/hitters at UCLA, on the first undefeated collegiate volleyball team in history. That began a strong sense of domination in us that carried over as the best team on the beach. Could we have continued as the best? Who knows? One advantage we had was playing in an era when blocking over the net was not allowed.

Most teams served Sinjin, since he didn't appear as powerful a hitter as Randy. I think that was a mistake—it played right into their strengths. Sinjin was a perfect passer and Randy had exquisite hands, so he was a much more accurate setter than Sinjin. Plus, with Randy not hitting, he could stay fresh all day long to block and jump serve—which were their greatest offensive weapons. But the biggest mistake in serving Sinjin was that you were serving to a tireless, tenacious sideout machine. He was really tough to beat.

While I admired Sinjin's efforts to promote the sport, I wasn't enamored of the way he and Randy played the game. They constantly bickered and whined about the referees' calls. One time Sinjin refused to come out on the court to play the finals of the winners' bracket because he didn't like one of the linesmen chosen to officiate the match. Finally, the head ref started awarding points to the opposing team. After eleven points, Sinjin finally stepped onto the court.

They also took every opportunity that came their way to belittle their opponents. If they happened to lose, there was always an excuse ready— some kind of injury or another—but never an admission that they were outplayed. I just felt their behavior was unbecoming to the best team in the world.

Although I believed I could have beaten them if I had found the right partner, their reign between 1986 and 1990 was undisputed. Only Tim Hovland and Mike Dodd seriously challenged them. If I wanted to be on the number-one team, that meant taking them down. And kept me searching for the right guy, even though the top players were firmly committed to each other. My indoor obligations scared away the best players.

From the get-go in 1983, Sinjin was an integral part of the AVP. He was on the board of directors, and was never short on ideas of how to grow the sport or on how to implement them. He worked closely with the AVP's executive director, Leonard Armato, and also signed a contract with Armato to represent him as an agent.

A big problem with the AVP board of directors, as we certainly recognize now, was that its members were comprised strictly of active players. Young guys in their twenties who play volleyball for a living aren't the best qualified to run a business. Consequently, as executive director, Leonard Armato ran the AVP pretty much as he pleased. Although the tour became more successful each year, questions eventually arose from the ranks and the board about some of Armato's dealings. Questions about the various and entangled relationships Armato had constructed between the AVP and the corporate sponsors. Questions about the relationships between the AVP and Armato's own company. Questions about relationships between the AVP and some of Armato's clients, including Sinjin and Randy. Some members of the board not only hadn't known about those relationships, but also probably couldn't have understood them if they had. That was one of their shortcomings. Nonetheless, questions had arisen.

In 1989 the annual election for board members was held. Sinjin, finishing fourth, didn't get voted back on to fill one of the three vacancies. He was furious about that, as well as about one new member, Tim Walmer, who had actively campaigned for votes. Not against the bylaws but not kosher, Sinjin felt.

I was one of three board members voted on. Immediately, we started asking hard questions about Armato's relationships. The result was that Armato promptly resigned from his position as executive director. Outraged again, Sinjin felt that we had scared away the guy who had built the AVP to its level of success. In response, Sinjin led a recall vote of the three new board members, who included myself.

Fiery letters to AVP players were sent—Sinjin accusing, we three defending. What a waste of time! That next year was one of the worst of my life. In the end, we were not recalled and Sinjin had lost his influence in the AVP. My sense is that he felt people were out to get him, so he looked elsewhere to be a factor in the sport's destiny.

That place was with the FIVB and Ruben Acosta. Sinjin had already gotten close to Acosta during the Rio de Janeiro tournaments, and now he was a valuable resource for Acosta's plans for beach volleyball. It also coincided with Sinjin and Randy's waning career as the kings. Since the middle of 1991, they hadn't been able to win tournaments anymore. Wisely, they turned more and more to competing on the FIVB tour.

In the early 1990s their presence on the FIVB tour began to fester among the rest of the AVP players. First, we were required by our sponsor, Miller Brewing, to play in all our tour stops, so skipping an event for an FIVB tournament was essentially breaching the contract. Sinjin and Randy ignored it and a fine was levied on them by the AVP, though the AVP never followed through. Second, there were many American teams better than those two guys on the AVP tour but they never got the special FIVB invitations to play in the international tournaments. Only Sinjin and Randy did.

It was clear that Sinjin Smith and Randy Stoklos were the recipients of Acosta's blessing. He needed some big-time American names on his FIVB tour and he had two of the biggest. Although we were unhappy with that, we were very happy about Acosta's and Sinjin's efforts to get beach volleyball accepted into the 1996 Atlanta Olympics as a medal sport.

We were thrilled with the news of Atlanta, but the announcement of Acosta's qualification format for the Games stirred up a whole new nest of hornets. According to the plan, AVP players would have to play in a number of FIVB events in order to qualify for the Olympics. We felt that we were being coerced into playing, and supporting, Acosta's international tour and his designs (imaginary or not) on controlling beach volleyball worldwide. At the same time, our mandatory attendance at FIVB events would weaken our own tour here in this country—our first allegiance. It soon became a standoff. Could the AVP players, the best in the world, possibly be denied the chance to play in the Olympics? Because of politics?

The acrimony continued until December of 1994, when a compromise was reached. The AVP would recognize the FIVB and USA Volleyball (USAVB) as official governing bodies of the sport. In turn, the AVP players would be allowed to compete in the Atlanta Olympics—provided they conformed to the FIVB qualification guidelines. Still, the controversy and vitriol heated to a full boil. I would be right in the middle of it. Sinjin would be as well.

Kent Steffes and I continued to hone our game to a fine edge. A deadly one. Both of us sided out well. We played a very balanced game and minimized our mistakes. Winning and confidence feed on each other, and between the end of the 1991 season and 1996 we had both in abundance—and a killer instinct. Our great year in 1992 proved to be no fluke. We went on to win eighteen of twenty-three events in 1993 and seventeen of twenty-one in 1994.

In all fairness, the talent pool on the tour wasn't as deep then. Often we would trounce teams 15–1 or 15–2 in the quarterfinals. That doesn't happen today. With more and more powerful and aggressive jump serves, as well as the addition of top-level international players, anything can happen in the early rounds of a tournament. Now more than ever, every match is a tough one.

The stubbornness and persistence of Kent Steffes is second only to Sinjin's—but a close second. That's an asset in competition. I can be just as stubborn while I'm competing, but volleyball is not a complex thing. Real life, with all its social, cultural, and political issues, is full of complexities often defying simple answers. Kent is very bright and informed—he's a tough guy to argue with—and he's convinced that his answer is the right one and the only one on every issue. I view most issues as having much more subtlety, and I think that the other point of view usually has some validity. Life requires tough choices and a lot of times those choices require trade-offs.

Politically, Kent is very conservative. He wouldn't have been invited to stand up with Newt Gingrich at the 1992 Republican National Convention if he weren't. I'm fairly conservative but not on every issue. I favor capital punishment, but I'm middle-of-the-road on abortion—opposed to making it too convenient, but not for outlawing it except in the third trimester. A sperm newly united with an egg is not the same as a newborn infant, in my mind.

I try to stay abreast of what's going on in the world. Rarely do I read fiction anymore. I prefer to read about current events. Two books that I recently read and found enlightening were *The Death of Common Sense* and *Out of Africa,* written by an African-American who has some incisive comments on racism in America as compared with that which exists in Africa.

In 1997 President Clinton suggested that we concentrate on racial issues in town meetings and make it a topic of national debate. I think we'd be better to not focus on race as an issue but to concentrate instead on kindness, just treating people a little better every day, with a smile and a hello—all people, regardless of their color. My preference is not to divide people by race, but to divide them into the kind and decent on the one hand and the mean and indecent on the other.

Having two young boys and witnessing the recent spate of teenage shootings in public schools, I obviously have a concern about weapons. I wish we had a giant magnet to suck them all up and do away with them. We'd certainly be better off if we didn't have so many around. But that isn't going to happen. Guns have been around a long time. It's the employment of them that has changed. In the West during the 1800s, families had firearms and kids had access to them, but they didn't use them on their teachers and classmates. I can only conclude that kids were better grounded.

There's no way to simplify it. The best answer is to have parents spend more time with their kids to give them keener moral compasses, but that's not as easy as it sounds either. We live in a complex world.

Kent and I may not have been aligned on every political issue, but we were very in sync on the sand. We each won about $450,000 in prize money in both 1993 and 1994. I earned about $500,000 each year in endorsements as well—making a million bucks a year to play beach volleyball was unbelievable. For Kent and me, things were only looking up. Until 1995. Shortly after the season began, Kent tore the labrum in his shoulder and had to undergo surgery. That forced him to miss three and a half months of the tour.

I decided to hook up with Scott Ayakatubby, a guy loaded with physical talent. We had a lot of success that season, but I informed him up front that I would go back to Kent when he returned from his injury. Kent was my partner and I felt obligated to reunite when he got healthy. I did.

When Kent returned we played in four tournaments, taking a third, second, first, and fourth. That wasn't as good as Scott and I had done—we'd won half the events we entered. With only three tournaments remaining, I was shooting for the Miller Lite Cup, an award for the player who accumulated the highest point-total for finishes in a season. It meant about $125,000—and both Mike Dodd and Mike Whitmarsh were catching up to me in points, so I told Kent I was going to play the last three with Ayakatubby. I was also concerned about the long-term outlook for his shoulder. We agreed to huddle after the season and see how his shoulder was doing. If it became as strong as before, we would stay together for the 1996 season and the Atlanta Olympics.

In January of 1996 Kent and I got together. He was playing like his old self, so I kept my commitment. We would be partners for 1996 and the Atlanta Olympics—if we could qualify.

The first half of the 1990s saw a steady growth of popularity in beach volleyball. It was overseen by Jeff Dankworth, who had replaced Leonard Armato as executive director in the fall of 1990 and stayed until early 1995. The previous year the Northridge earthquake had hit. It was so traumatic to Dankworth and his family, with their home having been just a mile or two from the epicenter, that they decided to move to Reno, Nevada. When the commute to L.A. proved too much, Dankworth resigned and was replaced by Jerry Solomon, who'd been, among other things, my agent since 1986.

Jerry and his right-hand man, Lon Monk, and I had always had a great relationship. For many years Jerry had been chief operating officer of ProServ, a sports marketing company, before he decided to form his own sports marketing company, P.S. Star Games, in 1995. When Jerry took the job as executive director of the AVP as well, we, of course, had to terminate our business relationship. To continue would have been a conflict of interest. Subsequently I signed with Craig Tartasky, after Solomon had endorsed him as a capable replacement.

At the time, I was torn about Jerry's decision to take the job since I would be losing a great agent. However, he looked good on paper as a guy who could lead the AVP to new heights.

The general consensus among the players was that Dankworth had done a good job. After all, the prize money had increased during his tenure and that's what players cared about most. We still hadn't learned about fiscal responsibility at the board level, even after going through the Armato ordeal. Although I was only on the board for one year beginning in 1990, a cast of players came after me. Probably no player board member was ever totally qualified to sit in that position. In truth, players sometimes didn't know what questions to ask. Because of that inexperience, directors weren't very firm in holding AVP management's feet to the fire. A twenty-five- or thirty-year-old player who has never held a full-time job doesn't command much respect as a board member. Players could be bamboozled or intimidated—and they were. At times, we tried to find businessmen to sit on our board but we never found any who were interested.

The case of Dankworth illustrated the problem. For the last two years he worked, he never collected the money he was owed, and it was never entered on the books as the $500,000 liability it really was. At least another $250,000 was owed to financial consultants. So Dankworth left the AVP with somewhere between a half million and a million dollars in debt—according to Dankworth.

However, Solomon would later say that the debt was actually $1,500,000 when he took over in mid-1995. The unfortunate thing is that the amount of the actual debt when Solomon took over the reins is still unclear. Until that's known—if it ever will be—it remains difficult to judge Dankworth's and that board's performance.

What is quite clear from today's perspective is that the prize money grew too quickly, at the expense of the AVP paying its bills. The prevailing attitude of the administrators—and players went along smilingly—was that prize money showed growth so everything was fine. But the unpaid bills kept mounting year after year without the executive director being held answerable for it. Some of the time the right questions weren't asked.

And when they were, the guys in charge would often get indignant and defensive. The result was that the board of directors, made up of players, never really knew what the numbers were. And even if they did know, what would they—or we—have done anyway? We just continued to go along with things. From late 1996 on, the situation grew progressively worse.

Playing on the beach requires a different kind of physical conditioning than indoors. In large part, I quit playing indoors in 1992 because I wasn't sure I could take five hours a day, five days a week, jumping on a hardwood floor anymore. I know my body couldn't withstand that abuse today.

It takes a big adjustment for pro beach players to get into playing shape for indoors. More muscle and joint strength is required, so there's a lot more weight training and specialty work like plyometrics where various kinds of jump training are employed. On the other hand, indoor players would have trouble stepping out on the beach and playing up to seven or eight games on Sunday to win a tournament. Stamina is imperative. Although physically stronger, most hardcourt players would end up prostrate on the sand, their bodies locked in one big, cramping knot.

I've cramped a few times in my life. The first time was during college and the second was in 1985 in Clearwater, Florida, during one of the hottest tournaments I ever played in. It was in midsummer and the heat and humidity were ungodly. An inferno on the beach.

Guys were keeling over left and right on Sunday morning—even refs were passing out. When Mike Dodd and I walked out on the court to play against Sinjin and Randy for the finals of the winners', just standing in the sun made my heart pound so hard that I thought it would come right out of my chest. I'd never felt that before.

We played, but after every four or five plays or so, we had to stop and get off the court. The four of us would scurry to get under an umbrella, then throw towels soaked in ice water over our heads. Then back for another four plays, and over to the shade and ice water. At one point Randy walked over to the medical tent where a huge cooler full of ice was sitting. He laid back on the table, emptied the cooler of ice on himself, and just stayed there covered with ice.

Unfortunately we lost 15–13, and thirty minutes later had to step back into hell for the finals of the losers. Sinjin and Randy had a room overlooking the tournament and we could see them on their balcony looking down at us playing, cackling at our fate. It was mostly in fun—more for them than for us, admittedly—and we made a few obscene gestures in their direction from time to time.

We were playing Andy Fishburn and Jay Hanseth, when Hanseth took a time-out in an effort to combat the heat. Jay had really thick, black hair and he felt that his head was absorbing too much heat. Somehow he had gotten hold of some aluminum foil and during the time-out he constructed a type of cap to deflect the sun's rays, poking holes in it for ventilation. Back on the court, standing in that shimmering heat, was this guy playing with a shiny, aluminum skullcap. This ultimate baked potato was one of the oddest sights I've ever seen.

We beat them and then had to face a cooled-off Sinjin and Randy once again. We built a small, early lead and I felt the first twinges in my legs— a bad sign. A couple of plays later, one of my thighs locked into a tight contraction. Soon the other leg went. It was duck soup for them after that. They finished us off 15–10.

One of the common remedies for cramping to come out of volleyball lore was to drink a couple of beers to loosen up your muscles. A few times in my career I was cramping so badly that I tried it since I would hate to ever default, and that was the most immediate remedy available. Some guys on the tour inject IV bags to stave off cramps during tournaments, but I've never done that. I feel that they're an unfair performance enhancement.

The last time I used the old beer technique was in 1996 and it caused quite a flap. It happened in a sweltering tournament in Belmar, New Jersey, where I cramped and had a few beers to loosen myself, and keep me loose, during the game. Kent and I proceeded to win the tournament against Scott Ayakatubby and Brian Lewis in a double finals. However, NBC got wind of it and reported on the update that I'd had fourteen beers, instead of a few.

A lot of controversy ensued because the numbers were so exaggerated. Our CEO, Jerry Solomon, thought the wrong message was being sent. The AVP board agreed, so we voted to forbid alcohol consumption during tournaments. As a board member, I voted for the ruling as well.

I realize that my image as a role model is important. I also am aware that for most of my playing career I've carried myself with a pretty high level of comportment. But I'm not perfect.

In 1989 I experienced one of the most enraging losses of my life—and exhibited behavior that shocked a lot of people. Brent Frohoff and I were going tooth and nail against Sinjin and Randy in the finals of an AVP tournament in Rhode Island. It went to a final game to seven points, and we were tied 6–6. We served, Brent dug a ball, I set it, and he killed it for the win. Except the ref, Ed Winchester, said my finger had touched the attack on my block, which made for four hits—a violation—and a sideout for the other guys.

But I never touched it. It was bad enough to lose, but to lose on a violation you never made was the worst. My instincts took hold and I grabbed the net with both hands, yanking it down with every ounce of my rage. The entire net and standards collapsed to the ground like a tree being felled. And Winchester came down with it too—although he was unhurt—on national TV! The volleyball world, and a lot of viewers, were shocked.

How did I feel about it later? The same as I'd felt the moment I pulled it down—great.

CHAPTER FIFTEEN

ATLANTA BEACH

Dad! Dad! The pool's closed!"

I had been looking up at the thousands of fans descending toward the court and at the towering six-foot-eleven figure of basketball-legend-turned-sports-announcer Bill Walton struggling to get a microphone in front of me. But it was Kristian's voice that got my attention. Instantly his disappointment brought me from the heights of ecstasy down to terra firma. Kristian didn't care about the Olympic gold medal. All he wanted was for us to go to the kids' pool. It immediately put things in perspective.

Still, it was awesome. I felt an elation not only for myself but for the sport as well. A lot of people had played, and made contributions, to the game since the first beach volleyball was served in 1930, and here I was the beneficiary of all that history.

Not that I felt unworthy. Beginning in 1995 my daily regimen leading up to Atlanta was the most arduous I ever followed. Here is an example of a day's training taken from my workout diary during that period:

- one-half hour of Inflex stretching; six minutes of stances
- sets of twenty-five maximum block jumps—both standing and one-step sideways—to a total of 350 in about thirty minutes
- practice: drills and scrimmage, three hours
- lunch

- rest
- strength train:
    - five minutes of rowing, at ninety-five percent maximum rate
    - three sets of ten—forward and backward—lunges, with various dumbbells
    - five sets of eight jumps onto boxes, up to forty-three inches high with up to thirty-five-pound dumbbells
    - eight sets of three to five clean lifts, from 60 to 105 kilos
    - four sets of twenty plyometric pushups, supersetted with four sets of eight to twelve incline bench presses, with dumbbells up to seventy pounds
    - four sets of eight to twelve dips, with up to fifty pounds strapped on
    - eight sets of various dumbbell curls, various weights
- ten minutes of various abdominal drills
- rest
- jump serve workout:
    - up to 160 jump serves of various types, some for accuracy and some for maximum power
- dinner
- sleep

At the end of those workout days I was exhausted. After we put Kristian and Kory to bed, Janna and I would often lie in bed and watch a *Seinfeld* or *Cheers* rerun. I still enjoy that—ending the day on a happy note.

I slept well in that period. I knew how important that rest was to winning. I also knew that the upcoming competition could greatly change my sleeping patterns. It had happened before. A big match, won or lost, could keep my mind doing instant replays for hours, unable to switch it off. For Atlanta I decided to make sure that I would be properly rested, which meant being able to sleep after a match no matter what happened during it. I sought out some expertise.

I visited a psychologist who specialized in biofeedback. I told him I wanted a stress-management tuneup, mostly for the occasional nights when I would wake up and start thinking too much, racing from thought to thought.

He taught me some relaxation techniques. One way he suggested to keep my mind from racing was to picture the most relaxing environment or situation I could think of. For me, that was the Outrigger Canoe Club in Honolulu. I'd envision my kids playing at the edge of a pristine Pacific Ocean, or I might be enjoying a friendly volleyball game or having a leisurely lunch on the oceanfront terrace—a totally relaxing day.

I also learned some breathing exercises to release tension as well as help me get back to sleep in the middle of the night. I would have to use them several nights in Atlanta, particularly the night following the fabled match we played against Sinjin Smith and Carl Henkel.

As the months ticked down to Atlanta, the animosity between the FIVB and the AVP seemed to grow. The fact that Sinjin and his partner, Carl, had already earned an Olympic berth by virtue of their top finish on the separate FIVB tour rankled us. The fact that Sinjin was very close to Acosta, and a direct influence on him, rankled us even more. The few times Sinjin and Carl played in AVP events, they'd gotten crushed. Now they were taking one of the three spots that we felt all American teams should have had a shot at—a spot that should have been filled by a much better team, or at least by a team that earned the spot by beating the other best American teams.

We let the media know our feelings and the other side did the same. I, in particular, let my convictions be known to the press at every occasion I was asked. Even my dad—a very strong-willed, opinionated man—got into the fray. As a form of protest against the FIVB qualification policies, he opted not to come to the Atlanta Olympics. Predictably, Ruben Acosta and Sinjin countered with their own beliefs.

Still, if we wanted to play in Atlanta we had to jump through the official hoops. That meant playing in a week-long qualifying tournament, the Olympic Trials, in Baltimore in early June of 1996. Looking back, that competition was even more stressful than the week at the Olympics. The thought that something could go haywire—an injury, for example—wore on my nerves constantly.

In fact, when Mike Dodd and Mike Whitmarsh beat Kent and me 15–7 in the winners' bracket and went on to clinch the first of the two Olympic berths still open, there were many angst-filled moments I had to contend with. They had played an impeccable match. Now Kent and I had one last chance. We had to face Adam Johnson and Randy Stoklos on the final day, June 9, to see who would be the third American team in Atlanta. Unfortunately, Stoklos had landed on a ball in warm-ups the day before and sprained his ankle. Although he put forth a valiant effort, the injury affected his play. We breezed to a 15–2 victory and a ticket to Atlanta. Now we could breathe a little.

Six weeks later we were in Atlanta. This time I was going to do the Olympics my way. We rented a private home so our whole family could stay together, including Janna, our kids, my mother and Janna's parents, and my sister Kati. We had a great time there. At the playing site there was a water park and the kids played there every afternoon. We had home-cooked meals. I put my relaxation techniques to work. I slept well.

Sleeping well at the Olympics was unusual. In the Olympic Village the excitement level is so high, everyone is so amped-up, that no one is ever thinking of sleep. Also, a lot of athletes finish their competition early and after that they are out to have a good time, which is what the Olympics are also about. However, when you're still competing and everyone else is partying, it's not such a good time. In Seoul in 1988, our USA Men's Team was housed next to the Dutch dorm and those people were partying and coming in at three in the morning, making some awful noise. I didn't sleep very much that week.

I warned Kent about the rest problem in the Village. He tried to stay there anyway, but after three or four days he finally had to move to a hotel in order to get some sleep.

Things were lively at the beach volleyball stadium as well, aptly called Atlanta Beach. The daily sellout crowds of eleven thousand fans were a testament to people wanting to enjoy an Olympic event in a more relaxed atmosphere. And not just by watching. They dressed in beach shorts, danced in the stands to hot music, did the wave and the Macarena, and drank beer and margaritas under the sun. It was the coolest scene in the Games and the media hyped it as such.

As far as our playing, the week went smoothly until what everyone felt was the highlight of the event—our match against Sinjin and Carl. Given all the acidic rhetoric that had gone back and forth, it seemed fitting that we would face each other. I was in for a surprise. They played great. In fact, we were behind most of the match and barely escaped defeat, 17–15.

Of course, the media loved it and I felt obliged to give particular credit to both of them for their impressive performance. I had been too harsh, too critical of their earlier play, because of my frustration with the Olympic qualification process—even though they'd been terrible in AVP competitions. However, in Atlanta the FIVB rules were different than ours and they used a different ball. More importantly, Sinjin rose to the occasion. But I still didn't condone the qualification process that he and Acosta had imposed on beach volleyball.

In light of that, at the press conference following the match I expressed my disdain for the blatant cheering of Malu Acosta (Ruben's wife) for Sinjin during our match, as well as every other time he played. To hear her screeching voice—"Go Sinjin!"—so audibly was way out of line. And distasteful. She represented the FIVB and all volleyball players worldwide. It was tantamount to Hillary Clinton coming to the Olympics and cheering for just one American athlete against all the rest.

The press seemed to particularly enjoy my imitation of her shrill voice. About five minutes later, guess who walked into the press conference? Malu, a Mexican woman fashionably dressed and richly bejeweled as usual, strolled up to me with a big smile on her face and said, "Congratulations, Karch."

Later I passed her in the hallway and she said, "Don't I get a kiss on the cheek?"

I gave her a quick peck, wondering if she saw me after the final point of the Sinjin match when I looked up toward her sitting in the official box and let out my best primal scream—something best not repeated. I never spoke to Ruben Acosta during the event.

After the Olympic Trials and that match against Sinjin, the finals seemed almost anticlimactic. Kent and I would face Mike Dodd and Mike Whitmarsh, and it seemed like the pressure was off all of us since we had accomplished our two big goals: an all-American finals and an all-AVP finals.

Still, the excitement started mounting. But we all felt bad that my dad and my younger sister, Kristi, were not there to share this time with us. We missed them. My mom, in particular, was really disappointed that my dad wasn't there. The night before the finals I called and asked him, "Why don't you come for the last match?"

I could tell he was tempted. "I don't want to come if it's going to put more pressure on you guys."

"I don't think it will at all," I responded.

"Well, it's your call," he told me.

"Come on then. And bring Kristi too."

I made plane reservations for them to take a red-eye flight into Atlanta. My sister had just arrived from New York and was on vacation with a friend in Santa Barbara. My dad began a frantic search to track her down, since the flight would leave L.A. in about five hours. He found her, and all three of them made the flight.

Early Sunday morning my mom picked them up and brought them back to the house at about the time we were all waking up. We all sat down for breakfast as a reunited family. I had my normal good-luck breakfast— oatmeal.

After the meal everyone left, except Janna and the kids. Janna had made a huge pasta dish a few nights before and one of the many lessons I learned from my dad was to finish things before they go to waste. So I finished the pasta for lunch, took a rest, then Janna drove me to the stadium.

Before the finals I felt pretty loose, joshing around with Dodd and Whitmarsh before warming up. Being buddies, we were all pretty relaxed.

I wasn't sure whether we'd win or not. I did know that they had kicked our butts in the Olympic Trials where they had played a perfect match. Also, they had beaten us twice in an AVP event in Maine two weeks before. Still, Kent and I usually came out on top and I felt pretty good about our chances.

We walked out to the practice court to stretch and warm up. I heard someone calling me from behind the barrier that surrounded the court and then I saw this huge red-headed guy—one of very few people tall enough to look over the fence. It was Bill Walton. Since he was doing the court-side commentary, he wanted to get a few comments from me on how we planned to play the match.

After I'd warmed up, we walked out on the center court. Over ten thousand fans were waiting. "Karch, is that a familiar face I see up there?" Mike Dodd called over to me, pointing to the VIP section.

Sure enough, he had seen my dad. Actually, my dad was hard to miss, all decked out in his AVP garb, but I hadn't told anyone he was there and it wasn't until later that I learned how he had managed to get a seat in the VIP section.

Since our arrival in Atlanta we had been trying to get to know some of the ushers so that we could have our immediate family seated in the VIP section even though they didn't have official passes. On the day of the finals they were able to enter the section as normal. Except for my dad. Since the guards hadn't seen him earlier in the week, they weren't buying his story that "I'm Karch Kiraly's father!"

It went on until an African-American official showed up to see what was going on. In discussing the problem, it was discovered that he actually spoke Hungarian—"one of the most useless languages in the world," according to my dad. Well, they hit it off and that got my dad his VIP seat.

The only fault I could find in that day was the drizzle, which continued the entire match. Everything else went according to script—almost perfectly. Kent and I would have the match of our season. It was a good day to have it on.

Mike Whitmarsh is six-foot-seven and the best blocker on the beach. He can get his hands way over the net and is very adept at reading where hitters like to direct their attack. Mike Dodd is six-foot-five and a great digger. Long and lean, he can cover a lot of ground behind Whitmarsh. Their blocking and digging combination made for a formidable defense, which was their strength. Their strategy in the finals was the same one they had used against us all year. Start serving me—the older guy—and see if I gave them points. If that didn't work, they would switch to serving Kent.

I had hurt my back earlier in the year, and when I had to face the big barrier of Whitmarsh's hands, I used a lot of soft placement shots because I couldn't hit the ball hard. I resorted to those shots right away, and they were effective. Even though Whitmarsh stuffed some back on our side of the net, Kent and I made some phenomenal saves to keep the ball alive, then kill it. In fact, later that evening Mike Whitmarsh's brother, Russ, came up and said, "When you made that cover of yourself in the first game to save a point, I knew you guys were going to be unbeatable. I've never seen a play like that."

He was referring to a spike I made at the net at about the middle of the court. Whitmarsh blocked it back almost to my sideline and about four feet off the net. I turned and lunged in a full-out dive and somehow got it up. Kent set me and I put it away, preventing them from getting a precious point. Kent also made several great saves that had looked like sure points for them.

We opened up with a 6–0 lead in the first game and never looked back, winning it 12–6. Since the format was two-out-of-three games to twelve points, we needed one more game. We started well again. In the second game, two plays stick out in my mind. Kent dug a ball and I scrambled all the way to the back fence, hoping just to save it and bump it anywhere on our side of the net. My bump dropped about twenty feet from the net. Kent took a swing at it and somehow the ball hit the top of the net, teetered for a moment, and rolled over on their side for a point.

A while later I dug a ball and Kent bumped about a forty-foot set that landed almost on the net. Whitmarsh wasn't ready for such a great set, but he still tried to rush to the net to put up a block on me. I saw he was late and blasted it off his hands for another point. That's the kind of day it was for Kent and me. Everything fell our way.

The match was unusual in another sense. There was no screaming or intimidating going on through the net, as in the Smith and Henkel match. We were even talking and complimenting each other when someone made a good play. Earlier that day I had been daydreaming a little and fantasized about faking an injury during the finals at a tie-score, somehow creating a situation where all four guys would get a gold medal. Just a daydream, but that's how I felt.

The only moment of doubt came late in the second game when the two Mikes made a little run at our lead. If their defense happened to click in, they could get on a roll and snatch a victory out of any jaws of defeat. I'd seen them do that before. At 11–6 and match point, I gave Kent a good set and he ripped it, only to have Dodd pop it up and put it away for a sideout. That gave me a shiver of fear.

But not for long. Soon after, Kent blocked Whitmarsh for the final point and we won the gold, 12–6. It was fitting for Kent to make the final play because he had clearly been the best player and MVP of the Olympic beach competition.

When the last ball touched the ground, I tackled Kent in jubilation. We got to our feet and ran to the net where the four of us had a group hug and congratulated each other.

That moment was special for me in a different sense, compared with my other two Olympic finals. Here were four guys who had played so hard and done so much to get to this ultimate moment—for themselves and for their sport. Four buddies. Four beach volleyball players.

It was mind-boggling. Thousands of people were jostling for autographs. After Walton interviewed me, we were called to the awards ceremony on center court. During the ceremony a contingent of rowdy fans were doing AVP cheers and booed Ruben Acosta when he was introduced. It was Juan Antonio Samaranch who draped the medals around our necks—apparently something he rarely did, but it was a sign of the positive impact beach volleyball had made in the Games. Acosta handed each of us a bouquet of flowers, which I soon put at my feet, wanting to have my hands free to applaud the other two teams when they got their medals. Some people viewed that as an intentional slight to Acosta, but that's not how I meant it at all.

As our national anthem was playing, I turned and saw tears streaming down Kent's face. Aside from my marriage and having kids, the three greatest moments of my life have happened on that Olympic stand, though the emotions were different each time. L.A. was ecstasy. Seoul was relief. This was accomplishment.

Since the pool was closed, we went back for a low-key dinner. Then Janna, my sisters, and I went to a party put on by one of Kent's sponsors. We didn't stay too long, because we had to get up early to be on the *Today Show* the next morning.

When Katie Couric interviewed Kent and me, she put on one of my pink hats and turned the bill up. For several years I had been wearing a pink hat while playing, and it became something associated with me. Speedo was very happy about Couric wearing it as well. Within a few weeks Kent and I were on the *Tonight Show* with Jay Leno, and we also did many other TV and press interviews.

In Atlanta, beach volleyball had made a grand entrance on the world stage. The future looked as bright as a Southern California afternoon—for the sport and for me. Yet, for various reasons, our sport would not take advantage of our Olympic success. Trouble was already bubbling up from the bottom of the AVP although we as players didn't know it. A month later, the biggest adversity of my playing career hit me—a severe shoulder injury that would require major surgery, presenting me with the very real possibility that my career was over for good.

More strange things followed. Against my intuition and instincts, I joined the AVP board of directors and became embroiled in the financial fiasco the organization faced. We found out in 1997 that the AVP had been mismanaged, without the board's knowledge. Old friendships and relationships were broken. Even my former partner, Kent Steffes, filed a lawsuit against me. All this after the wonderful success of the 1996 Olympics.

Still, had I been forced to end my volleyball career in Atlanta, or soon after, I would have walked away a happy man—an incredibly lucky man, in my mind. I was thirty-five. I had done pretty much all that was possible in over twenty years of playing the sport.

CHAPTER SIXTEEN

TRIALS

For thirty-five years of my life, I had enjoyed good health. Able to bang hundreds of thousands of balls and jump a couple million times, my body still held up. In part, I was lucky. But a lot of it was also genetic. My parents heal pretty quickly. I also had pretty good body control on the court and knew when a situation might cause an injury, so I was careful to avoid it. Over a good twenty years of full-out competition, I only broke a finger and a hand, and sprained each ankle six or seven times. For all I had put myself through, I had been blessed.

But it couldn't go on forever.

The Atlanta Olympic beach volleyball competition ended July 28, 1996. A month later I was playing in a big AVP tournament in Chicago, warming up for my second match on Friday morning and spiking a ball back and forth with Kent to get my shoulder warm. I had done that simple exercise more times than I could ever count, but now I felt a sharp pain in my shoulder every time I hit a ball. Sometime between our first-round game and the next game's warm-up, something in my shoulder had given out.

I didn't mention it to Kent. I tried to play through it but we finished poorly, getting fifth. On Monday I went to see my physical therapist, Randy Bauer, but therapy didn't really improve things. We played in one more special event two weeks after Chicago, the Texas Shootout, in Austin. My shoulder was still killing me.

So I did more physical therapy, trying to avoid surgery. Three weeks later I played one more exhibition match and the shoulder was, if anything, worse. It was time to delve further and an MRI showed that I had a torn rotator-cuff muscle—serious stuff for a volleyball player, as for any athlete whose sport requires overhead movement. Those particular muscles are very susceptible to movements like spiking and throwing. I immediately sought the opinions of the best doctors I could find, including Dr. George Thabit in San Jose, California. Thabit had worked wonders on many volleyball players—including repairing Kent's shoulder in 1995.

Kent's shoulder looked stronger than ever by nine months post-operation, evidence that compelled me to go with Thabit. His plan was to repair my shoulder arthroscopically if the tear wasn't too big. If it was more severe he would have to do open surgery. When he went in, he not only found a sizable tear—he could put his finger through it—but he found gobs of scar tissue as well.

First he cleaned up the scar tissue arthroscopically. He also shaved down the acromion of the shoulder blade to prevent future injuries, and he repaired a partially torn labrum.

Then he performed another procedure on me, which was only four or five years old and considered by some conservative doctors to be unproven. When Thabit examined me he found that my right shoulder joint was very loose from all the years of wear—a common condition in volleyball players. What happens is that the capsular membrane in the shoulder gets very stretched out with overuse. He felt that if I didn't get it tightened up, my prospects for reinjury would be significant.

Thabit was one of the pioneers of the procedure, called laser capsulorraphy, in which he runs a laser across the membrane. The heat of the laser shrinks the membrane, much like cellophane shrink-wrap. The goal was to tighten up the whole joint, effectively providing me a rebuilt shoulder—or at least a tighter, better one.

After that procedure Thabit came out, drenched in sweat, to tell Janna (who was in the waiting room) that he'd have to use the open, more invasive procedure to give my shoulder the strongest possible repair. He also said,

"Janna, I can't believe he was able to play so long with all the scar tissue I saw." He went back to work, cutting my shoulder open and tying together the two sides of the hole in my rotator-cuff. After three hours, he was done.

Thabit had given me a complete overhaul and I came out feeling very optimistic. I also thanked my lucky stars that the rotator cuff hadn't torn a month earlier—during the Atlanta Olympics.

I worked hard at therapy. Five days after the operation I started driving three times a week to Santa Monica to work with a physical therapist of Thabit's choice, Gail Wehner, seeing Bauer the other two or three days. I was hoping to be at full strength in three to four months. At the four-month mark it was progressing nicely. Then one day in late February I was practicing with Kent and dove for a ball, jamming the shoulder, and suddenly the pain came back.

I didn't know if it was a new injury or if I had only set myself back in therapy by overworking. What I did know was that it hurt more and more. The King of the Beach tournament in Las Vegas, the kickoff of the '97 season, was a few weeks away. It's not only a big event, but a fun one, where invited top players play with a different partner in every match, then individual results are totaled to determine the King of the Beach. I decided to play. I fooled myself into thinking that my shoulder would miraculously recover, that it wouldn't hurt. A mistake.

Thabit came to Las Vegas and examined me in my hotel room. He gave me some shots of Novocain and had me throw a ball in the hotel corridor. Still, he couldn't find what was ailing me. I went out Saturday morning and played horribly, not even qualifying for Sunday—an event I had won four times in its five-year history. I could swing about fifty percent of normal speed at best. My shoulder was killing me—enough to know that if I was going to have that kind of constant pain, my playing days were over.

In Las Vegas I was worried enough to tell Kent that I would probably miss some early tournaments. "You can find a temporary partner until I come back. Or you can decide you've had enough of me and my thirty-six-year-old shoulder and hook up with a new, permanent partner like Jose."

Obviously Kent now had doubts about my future. I was thirty-six, with a lot of miles on my body.

I flew home from Vegas, and up to San Jose the next day for another MRI exam. Thabit didn't see any new damage but said I needed to rest it. I called Kent and told him the news.

A few days later I got a call from Adam Johnson. "Karch, you wanna play together?"

"Why?" I was surprised.

"Because Loiola just dumped me."

"You're kidding! For Kent?"

"Yeah! Didn't you know?"

I suspected but hadn't actually heard yet. About twenty minutes later Kent called to give me the news. Alas, two more beach volleyball marriages had broken up.

Kent made a wise choice for a new partner—the new King of the Beach, Jose Loiola from Brazil, had won the event in Las Vegas. Loiola is six-foot-four and has an incredible jump and fast arm. A few years earlier, Randy Stoklos came up to me and said, "Don't take it personally, Karch, but I think Jose Loiola is the highest jumper on the beach I've ever seen."

I agreed. Or at least he's one of the highest in today's game. Emmanuel Rego, another Brazilian on the tour, looks like he jumps even higher. I don't jump as high as I did when I was twenty-five, but I've still got a decent jump. Mostly good genes, but when you get into your thirties your hope is not to lose any inches. Jose is twenty-eight years old, and with those hops it's clear why he has been selected Best Offensive Player on the AVP Tour the past few years.

During Kent's call we didn't discuss whether his partnership with Loiola was permanent or not. I just left it at that. The two dumpees, Adam and I, hooked up. Slowly, surely, my shoulder started feeling a little better every week in practice. After missing seven events, it was time to get back.

"You need to go out and play in competition," Thabit told me. "We need to find out if it's worse than before. And how it holds up weekend after weekend. It's time to test it."

Since Kent and Jose had won five of the first seven tournaments, I called him to verify what I already guessed. "I assume you're staying with Jose as a permanent partner, right?"

He said he was. Honestly, I would have liked to have had a shot—a one-or two-week trial—to see if I could play at my former level, even though I was pretty sure I couldn't at that time. But just a chance to dump myself perhaps, rather than be dumped. I had given him a chance in 1995 after his recuperation, and would have liked the same thing. But Kent was seven and a half years younger than I. It was no surprise that he dumped me.

In my first tournament with Adam we took a surprising third place, but it was with smoke and mirrors. I hit only one ball hard the whole weekend. The rest were shots. I felt a stab of pain on my one hard swing, but my shoulder still felt better than in Las Vegas.

Adam and I continued to play every weekend. It was an up-and-down road. Some weekends I could hit pretty hard, others I couldn't. And there were other frustrations. Sometimes I'd spike a ball and it would go three feet long or wide. It was like I no longer had control of where I was hitting it. In part, I didn't. I hadn't fully realized that I had a new anatomy—essentially a new shoulder—and I needed time to adjust to it. Also, I had moments when I'd forget to admit to myself that, despite the frustrations, my shoulder was feeling better every week.

The lowest point came when we played in Chicago. That weekend we lost to two teams who had never beaten me and we finished in seventeenth place—my worst finish ever in a major tournament. I played horribly. The games were close, but I hit a ton of balls into the net or out.

I came home feeling really down and told Janna, "Probably the next call from Adam will be the dump call." It never came.

But the thought was always in my mind, like a virus—maybe I couldn't come back. Most of the time I could ignore the doubts that lingered and I kept focused on my goal, but in Chicago it jolted me. There were doubts in other people's minds too. I'm sure that in the players' tent the scoop was, "Karch is done. Put a fork in him."

Reporters would interview me and usually begin with, "Common opinion seems to be that you'll never be the player you were." That gets old after a while, but there was some validity to it.

Adam and I never talked about alternatives. Guys might have been calling him to play for all I knew. That happens all the time. In fact, guys were calling me too, though I don't know why, since I was playing so inconsistently. The attitude on the tour is that if you don't call and ask, you'll never know if another guy will play with you. For some reason, Adam kept the faith.

Had Adam given me the dump call, I would still have continued. My plan was to give it my best effort for the season of 1997 as well as 1998. I knew that Kent had also gone through months of struggling with his shoulder. I would give it two years. Besides, Adam and I had taken a couple of thirds with me putting no heat on the ball. I figured that if I could improve at all, we'd have a reasonable chance to win again.

Soon after, the pain in my shoulder subsided dramatically and we won a tournament in Hermosa Beach. We beat almost all the top teams, and the light at the end of the tunnel was suddenly in view. The next weekend in Sacramento was doubly satisfying because we came through the losers' bracket in very hot weather to beat Kent and Jose 15–8 in the finals.

We won the next two tournaments as well. I knew I was back.

If that year of 1997 was my toughest one ever on the court, it also signaled my toughest year off it to date. The whole pro beach game gradually started to unravel and I got stuck in the middle of it.

In September of 1996, disregarding my intuition, which screamed not to do it, I begrudgingly allowed someone to nominate me for the AVP board election for the first time since 1991. My first tenure had been so distasteful that only the urging of my dad, Jerry Solomon, his assistant Lon Monk, and Dan Vrebalovich (president of the board)—as well as that of many players—persuaded me to run again. Their reasoning was that a player of my stature was needed for the sport's credibility. I accepted because I felt a sense of obligation. However, I had no sense at all what troubles were brewing when I joined. Nor the hundreds of hours of service I would eventually volunteer—time away from family, shoulder rehab, and training—in order to get sued personally by a player who felt that I was to blame for the mistakes made by the AVP. It was crazy, and no fun.

In 1996 the media coverage of beach volleyball at the Atlanta Olympics was tremendous. The media seemed to love the fun-filled, relaxed atmosphere of Atlanta Beach and talk was that this sport was ready to boom. Though NBC had curtailed its coverage of live AVP events that summer, we assumed that was because its schedule was filled with the Olympic Trials and the Olympics themselves.

The summer of 1996 ended in a bang, and for us AVP players it looked like the dawn of a new era of growth. How wrong we were.

Slowly, a quagmire of problems began to emerge. In July of 1997 it was discovered that the chief financial officer of the AVP had been embezzling funds. Payment of prize money for two tournaments had to be indefinitely postponed. Those events caused the board great concern, and we increased pressure on Solomon and Monk to provide a clear representation of the financial status of the AVP. Vrebalovich took the initiative after we felt we couldn't get any straight answers, spending a week in the AVP office taking a hard-and-fast look at the books. He came away with the almost-unbelievable news that we were $2.3 million in debt.

How did that happen? Especially when Solomon assured us that the debt was far less? We immediately set about finding out. As the board restricted and reduced management's ability to make unilateral financial decisions, it caused some uncomfortable moments between Solomon and me. Jerry wasn't happy about some of the restraints we as a board then put on him. For example, there was now a check-writing supervision over him. We wanted to know when, for how much, and to whom checks were being written. It would cause Jerry and me to gradually grow apart.

If I had to analyze the situation now, I would have to say that under Solomon we weren't managed in a fiscally responsible manner. Prize money had continued to escalate. Budgets weren't adhered to. Also,

Solomon had adopted the stance that the AVP must charge admission for every seat at every event. In his mind, that was a financial necessity—events are too expensive to run if we also forsake ticket revenues. I believe that's true, but we lost a lot of fans with our implementation of the policy, which included putting solid green fences up on Hermosa Beach. That was considered blasphemy by many. Those fans were used to coming to the beach with their beach chairs and enjoying the day close to the players and competition. Now there were ticket-takers, cordons, and bleachers. Much of the old intimacy was gone.

That stance would result in the AVP losing the Manhattan Beach Open—the Wimbledon of our sport. It caused a lot of discussion as well as questioning of Jerry's tactics. Reportedly, he dealt with the California Coastal Commission arrogantly, thinking he could call the shots. In turn, the Coastal Commission took the position that they didn't need or want our event. In the end, they won. We lost the Manhattan Open.

It became apparent that the AVP hadn't taken advantage of the great interest in the sport in Atlanta. Just as in the 1984 and 1988 Olympics, there was little or no plan in place to exploit our successes. Also, our tour relied heavily on the sponsorship of Miller Brewing Company and that was great as long as they stayed in the sport. But what if they pulled the plug?

The questions, and the friction, between the AVP and Solomon got worse. In late 1997 the Board decided to sever the AVP's relationship with Solomon. With the 1998 season around the corner, we needed someone to steer the ship. And quickly. Harry Usher, a sports promoter and business-man, was hired for ninety days to straighten things out. When he walked into the office and started investigating the AVP's financial state, he found an overwhelming morass. The financial records were a total mess, as were most other aspects of the business, including legal and administrative. Before he could straighten things out, he had to find out what he was deal-ing with. That alone took weeks.

In the meantime, creditors were calling to be paid. We did our best to stave them off and exert damage control—not wanting our dire straits to become common knowledge. But the AVP is a small world and soon word got out. Rumors began to fly and players were demanding to know what was going on.

Usher called several meetings with the players and informed them that things were indeed in bad shape. We had few alternatives. The debt was now at about two million bucks. To prevent bankruptcy we had to spend a lot less money in 1998, and also pay down our debt. That meant eventually cutting the prize money in half—to $1.2 million. It also meant still not being able to pay the prize money owed to us from the end of the 1997 season.

Kent Steffes, in particular, felt strongly that his unpaid prize money of $60,000 should be paid immediately—to the point that he began threatening to sue the AVP, and the board members personally. He also became one of the loudest critics of the AVP, including the board, and his criticism was cited by the press frequently.

Beyond cutting back our prize money, Usher felt that we as players had to do a better job of promoting our sport, that we especially needed to make Miller Brewing feel positive about our sport and our commitment to it. We agreed. Players would spend a lot more time going early to AVP events in order to take part in promotional and charitable appearances.

There were many times through 1998 when I wondered if I had made a huge mistake by accepting my position on the board. It had always been a thankless job. And now I faced the possibility of getting sued. Sure, I had been a player on the AVP, like scores of guys, but I had never run the organization. Several years earlier I had sat on the board for a year but that certainly shouldn't have put me in a position of responsibility for the AVP's later failure. In truth, all I ever wanted to be was a player.

For American male beach volleyball players, the Atlanta Olympics had sealed our reputation as the world's best. Undeniably the rest of the world had made strides to catch up, but a gold and silver medal were pretty convincing. On the women's side the fact that Brazilian teams won the gold and silver was equally convincing. The Brazilian women were the best.

In September of 1997, at the World Volleyball Championships held at UCLA, we American men got our wakeup call too. Two Brazilians, Para and Guilherme, took down Mike Whitmarsh and his new partner, Canyon Ceman, to win the event. A different Brazilian team had taken Adam and me out of the tournament earlier.

Our American reign over beach volleyball had ended. Our supremacy had been usurped and it looks as though the international field of competition will continue to level.

What I have come to realize is that the AVP game and the FIVB game are very different. It takes an exceptional beach player to be good at both. Again, I can use the case of Smith and Henkel. In 1996 and at Atlanta, they were very good FIVB players but mediocre AVP players at best. The ball itself made a huge difference. They had been using the lighter FIVB ball for several years, while we AVP players hadn't touched that ball in a whole year before Atlanta. With the FIVB's lax setting rules thrown in, we AVP players were in another arena. That's clearer today.

The 1998 AVP season began on shaky legs. Big pay cuts and rumors of the tour's demise made the whole atmosphere on the tour difficult. Crowds were no bigger than earlier years. And I was still tormented by my board position, fielding dozens of phone calls a week and attending meetings of hostile players and agents demanding simple answers to complex questions. Oh, just to be a player again.

As far as playing, I was excited about the season and was in exceptionally good shape to start it. I felt great at the King of the Beach event in Las Vegas, taking second. I'd even had a good shot at winning it, until Mike Whitmarsh's back injury forced him out of the tournament.

Adam and I had a good start, winning the first event in Tucson before stalling out. In some of the hotter-weather events, like in Florida, Adam had problems with dehydration and fatigue; in a couple of events I played poorly. Some people were asking if I was thinking about switching partners, but I never did. Adam stuck with me the previous year through my horrible shoulder problems, and I wanted to give us every opportunity to flourish.

Loiola and Steffes quickly became the dominant team, winning five of the first seven events. Then in early June their sudden breakup rocked the tour. Loiola decided to team up with his compatriot, Emmanuel Rego, and play with him through the Sydney Olympics. That made sense but left Kent suddenly out in the cold. Once again, the fickleness of beach volleyball partnerships was illustrated. Kent hooked up with Mike Whitmarsh.

In June, Adam and I got back on track with wins in Sacramento and Cincinnati. After Sacramento I saw the lawsuit that had been prepared by Kent Steffes's attorney. In actuality, Kent had two lawsuits: one against the AVP itself, demanding immediate payment of his overdue prize money, and one that accused the six AVP board members of having breached our fiduciary duties and duties of loyalty to the AVP during the eleven months between November 1996 and October 1997. In essence, he held that all of the AVP's financial problems were attributable to our actions and inactions during that period. The suit was actually a derivative action whereby Steffes, as a member of the AVP, essentially filed a claim on behalf of the AVP against its board of six directors.

Several weeks later three out of the five current board members—the three who were not named in the lawsuit—were given the task of carrying out an unbiased investigation to determine if indeed the six members named had committed the alleged transgressions. After a thorough investigation under the guidance of an attorney, they concluded that none of the accusations had enough merit to pursue the action, and that the directors had always acted in the best interest of the AVP, so the AVP should not file suit, but rather drop the case immediately.

However, in order to have the case dropped, the plaintiff—the AVP—had to file a motion with the court. Since the AVP at that time was out of money and already owed over $120,000 to its attorneys, the lawyers understandably hesitated to do the work without better promise of eventually getting paid. With no motion filed, the case continued and a trial date was set for late February 1999. In the meantime, we six accused began preparing our defenses with lawyers.

I was very disappointed about the lawsuit because I was never excited about joining the board in the first place. I did it for the love of the game and the sense of obligation that I felt. The result was that I spent hundreds of hours trying to help the AVP out of its troubles, and eventually I was obliged to pay thousands of dollars in attorney fees to defend myself in a legal mess. A thankless job is an understatement.

I was also chagrined because Kent and I had been great playing partners for a long time, and good business partners as well. Never bosom buddies, but I felt we shared a strong mutual respect. That's all changed. He pointed the finger largely at me and I didn't believe it was justified.

There was plenty of blame to spread around to many different parties for the problems of the AVP. My hope was that the blame game wouldn't be played and finger-pointing wouldn't accelerate, especially since it appeared that the AVP was moving forward to more solid financial ground. But, with lawsuits flying around, it became much harder to keep moving.

Indeed, some very bad news arrived in mid-August when Miller Brewing announced that it was not exercising its option for the 1999 season. To many that appeared to be the death knell for the AVP as we had known it for fifteen years.

Although the problems off the court continued to escalate, I reminded myself that there were a lot of things that were beyond my abilities to change. What I could control was my destiny on the court. Adam and I stayed focused and won the last three tournaments that we played together, until he injured his back right before the final two events of the season. Admittedly we were both disappointed. I didn't play in the next-to-last tournament, but I did play in the last one with Dain Blanton. We took a seventh.

The season ended in one more dramatic—and somehow fittingly symbolic event—which typified how fractured the beach game had become. During the last tournament in Muskegon, Michigan, a quarrel broke out in the players' tent between Kent Steffes and Brian Lewis. There had been no love lost between Steffes and Lewis in the past—in truth, Steffes's lawsuits had made him unpopular with many AVP players.

The result was thirty-one stitches in Lewis's face, courtesy of Kent's right-handed sucker-punch to the eye. The game had reached an all-time low.

The AVP also hit bottom soon after the season when its cash reserves ran out, and it was determined that the total debt was about $2,600,000. Plans were made to file for Chapter 11 under the bankruptcy laws, which would allow us some time to hopefully reorganize and somehow salvage things. Under that plan, a potential buyer of the AVP would most likely negotiate with creditors to retire the debt at a reduced percentage.

In November the AVP filed for Chapter 11 bankruptcy protection. Several investment groups and sports promoters approached the board to take over a business that was encumbered both before and after the filing.

Not surprisingly the various entities were very concerned about the AVP's financial position and about Steffes' lawsuits. They didn't want to take over a business that was encumbered with legal entanglements. They also viewed them as a divisive element amongst the players, as well as a formidable obstacle to potential corporate sponsors. We on the board of directors agreed. It remained to be seen how Kent Steffes would view it.

A proposal put forth in early January of 1999 by Spencer Trask Securities, Inc., a venture capital firm based in New York, appeared to be the firmest offer and the one the AVP, creditors, and players would support. They would commit to purchase the assets of the AVP and transfer them into a for-profit corporation, one *not* to include players on the board—which was certainly fine by me. Time was running short, but players remained hopeful because we all looked forward to the day when the Tour would establish a solid financial foundation, so it could begin thriving once again.

CHAPTER SEVENTEEN

BLESSED...AND LUCKY

Looking back at my life I am struck by how incredibly blessed, as well as lucky, I've been. First, to have met my life mate, Janna, and then to share two wonderful children with her is marvelous enough. In terms of volleyball, to have played with so many great players and win three gold medals, as well as all the beach tournaments I have won, is almost beyond imagination. I view it not just as a function of hard work and willpower—although those were big contributors—but that things also happened to fall my way. Just setting a dream for yourself and then working for it doesn't mean you'll get there by that alone. Sometimes a little luck is required.

In my case I had parents who gave me good genes—I could jump pretty high and had a resilient body—and they supported me financially when there was no other way to train full-time in my sport. I was also privileged to play during the game's golden era—admittedly, we helped to make it such an exciting period, both indoor and on the beach—but my timing happened to be perfect.

I virtually have no regrets in my playing career. There were plenty of losses, but those helped me to appreciate the wins that much more. I had to give up seven-and-a-half years of beach volleyball to play indoor for the USA Men's Team, but that afforded me two Olympic gold medals and a chance to be a part of the best team in the world. One thing I wish I could have done was to spend a year alone with Janna in Italy. To have been with her in such a romantic place would have been splendid, but the timing just didn't work out. The only real regrets I have are the two times I joined the AVP board of directors—and maybe those will seem as valuable experiences to me some day. They certainly haven't brought me anything good up to now.

I just turned thirty-eight and I feel like I'm still playing on a very high level. As long as I'm not suffering any pain, and as long as I enjoy playing, I want to keep competing. I expect to continue with Adam Johnson as my partner but, as we know in beach volleyball, that could change. The qualification process for the Sydney Olympics starts on January 1, 1999, and goes through June 2000. Selection of the two top teams will be determined by cumulative points from the best finishes in eight FIVB tournaments— there will be no Olympic Trials like in 1996. If the travel schedule becomes too burdensome for me, that will become a concern. I didn't get married to be away from my wife and kids for weeks on end. Hopefully the amount of travel won't be prohibitive.

I am a little befuddled with the sport right now. Both the indoor and beach game were much hotter properties in the late '80s and early '90s. The prize money for the 1998 AVP Tour was where it was about ten years before. The World League—the FIVB's premier indoor competition—is apparently suffering and, of course, both the USA Men's and Women's teams had disappointing finishes in the Atlanta Olympics. Recent reports have it that even the FIVB's beach tour will decrease its number of tournaments for the 1999 season. Hopefully these are only cyclical downturns and things will turn to the good before too long.

On the bright side, junior club volleyball—particularly girls'—continues to boom in this country, as well as women's collegiate volleyball. On the beach the recreational side of things is encouraging as more and more people are playing the game. One promising aspect I see in the pro beach game is the current attitude of the players. They are willing to spend time winning back fans, becoming more approachable and eager to give time promoting the sport.

My future in the game? I definitely want to stay in it, but I'm not sure what that means. Television broadcasting, clinics, and camps are all strong possibilities. I'm sure I'll eventually do more to help people learn about the game. I'd also like to carve out a niche for myself on the business side of the sport.

Right now I love living in San Clemente. Both Janna and I also love Santa Barbara, but as long as I have to travel a lot we'll stay here. Our kids love it here as well and that's important to us.

From time to time I'm asked about winning a fourth gold medal in Sydney, and setting Olympic history by accomplishing that over a sixteen-year period. I'm also aware that I am currently only four Open wins away from breaking Sinjin Smith's record. Truthfully I don't think about either very often. My greatest concern by far is the current survival of the AVP. I'd like to leave the game primed to grow and get better. That's the natural evolution of sports—more prize money and more television exposure. We've lost that momentum and I hope we get it back soon.

The great American volleyball player Gene Selznick was selected as an All-World indoor player in the 1956 World Championships. He also became the top player on the beach in his day. But he never got to play in the Olympics—either indoor or on the beach—never got to train full-time, never got the opportunity to earn his living playing the sport he loved. Through luck, timing, and hard work, I got to do all those things and more.

My biggest wish is to leave the game so that new players will have even more opportunities than I did. If anyone knows that's asking a lot, it's me. But like I say, I've been blessed—and lucky.

My dad in competition (far right). Hungary, 1954. *Courtesy of author's collection.*

Growing up in Michigan: My dad, mom, and me. Ann Arbor, Michigan, 1964.
Courtesy of author's collection.

My first lesson, age 6. With my dad on East Beach, Santa Barbara, 1967.
Courtesy of author's collection.

The Kiraly Family: (left to right) Karch, Toni, Las, Kristi, and Kati. Santa Barbara, 1976.
Courtesy of author's collection.

First trophy. My dad and I take third place in the Santa Monica B Tournment, 1976.
Courtesy of author's collection.

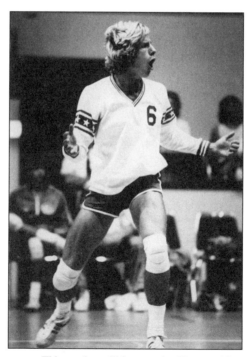

Thin . . . but still intense. An 18-year-old at
the Olympic Festival, 1979.
Photo by Doug Avery.

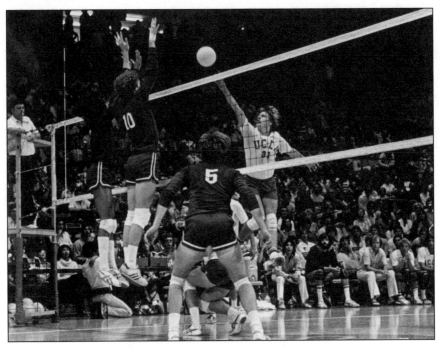

My college nemesis—the USC block. *Courtesy of UCLA.*

Still time for the beach game. Sinjin Smith
and I in 1980. *Photo by Doug Avery.*

Sinjin Smith and I after the San Diego Open, 1982.
Today, the two winningest players in history. *Courtesy of author's collection.*

Dusty Dvorak (#1) giving me a sweet set against
Brazil in the 1984 Olympic finals.
Courtesy of Allsport USA.

Steve Timmons and I enjoying a moment together—blocking a Cuban in 1986.
Courtesy of USA Volleyball.

Another gold! Celebrating after the final point in the gold medal match of the 1988
Olympics in Seoul. USA 3–Soviets 1.
Courtesy of Allsport USA.

Not an easy task—going against the big Soviet Block.
Courtesy of Allsport USA.

Me with the love of my life, Janna. *Courtesy of author's collection.*

For a while, the perfect partner. Kent Steffes and I after an AVP win in 1993. *Photo by Peter Brouillet.*

Steve Timmons and I were off to Italy in 1990. A lot of pasta, a lot of lira. *Courtesy of Allsport USA.*

During the salad days of the AVP. In 1994, there were little worries.
Courtesy of Peter Brouillet.

Defense wins games, 1994. *Courtesy of Peter Brouillet.*

Atlanta Beach, 1996. Our sport finally arrived—new
ball and all. *Courtesy of Peter Brouillet.*

In 1997, they started serving me more than my partner, Adam Johnson.
Courtesy of Peter Brouillet.

By the end of the 1997 season, my shoulder
was back. *Courtesy of Peter Brouillet.*

The off-season, doing what I like best—being with Kristian, Kory, and Janna.
Courtesy of author's collection.

Three Olympic golds—a lot of work and some luck too. One more in Sydney, 2000, would be a nice ending. *Courtesy of Peter Brouillet.*

GLOSSARY

AAA: The highest amateur rating in beach volleyball.

AVP: Asociation of Volleyball Professionals, founded in 1983, the official organization of the men's professional beach tour.

Block: A defensive barrier, made by a player's two hands, attempting to reject the spike of the opposing attacker. In the indoor game, a team tries to get two or three blockers against one attacker.

Blocking Rule Change, 1986: In today's beach game a blocker's hands can pass over the net. Before 1986 the rules wouldn't allow it, thereby diminishing the defense of beach volleyball and helping the smaller player.

Cross Court: A designated area diagonally opposite of where a player is on the court. For example, for a hitter on the left side of the court, the cross court is the right side of the opponent's court area.

Dig: The primary back court defensive maneuver in volleyball, similar to the forearm pass.

Dink: A little short shot over the block—a deceptive move used often in beach volleyball.

Dive: Where a player launches himself in the air, extending his body fully in an effort to lift the ball up in order to be played.

FIVB: Federation Internationale de Volleyball, founded in 1947, the official governing body of world volleyball, currently presided over by Ruben Acosta.

Jump Serve: A serve where a player essentially spikes the ball from behind the back line. Traveling much faster than other serves, the jump serve has become a powerful offensive weapon, revolutionizing the sport.

NORCECA: The North American, Central American, and Caribbean zone that determines Olympic qualification for the United States and other countries in the geographical area. NORCECA championships are held every two years.

Qualifier Tour: The AVP tour has a limited number of players (usually 48) that are automatically qualified to compete in tournaments—based on the preceding year's performance. A secondary tour allows for eight players over several tournaments to gain "exempt" status and enter AVP tournaments.

Serve Reception: The first contact by the receiving team after the ball is served. On the beach it is taken with a forearm pass—sometimes called a "bump."

Set: When a player takes the ball with both hands over the forehead in an effort to place the ball in a position to be spiked. On the beach the ball must come out of a player's hands cleanly, without spin, or a violation—a "throw"—is called.

Sideout: When a team receives the serve and kills the ball, it earns a sideout and the serve. A point can only be scored when a team serves, except in "rally scoring" where a point is earned on every serve. *Sideout* was the title of a 1986 feature film based on beach volleyball.

Spike: The term used for the attack in volleyball. With a firm, open hand a player contacts the ball, rolling the wrist over the top of the ball to create what is called topspin.

Triple Crown: The three ranking competitions of world indoor volleyball: Olympics, World Championships, and World Cup.

USAVB: See USVBA.

USVBA: United States Volleyball, the national governing body of the sport in this country. This organization changed its name to USA Volleyball (USAVB).

WPVA: Women's Professional Beach Volleyball Association, the women's version of the AVP that went out of business in 1998 due to internal and financial difficulties.

INDEX

ABOUT THE AUTHORS

Karch Kiraly resides in San Clemente, California. A professional beach volleyball player, Kiraly sealed his dominance of the beach game when he won the first-ever gold medal for the sport in the 1996 Olympics in Atlanta. Prior to his exploits in Atlanta, Kiraly was widely revered as the best indoor volleyball player in the world. A four-time All-American at UCLA, Kiraly went on to captain the USA Men's Team and lead his country to two Olympic gold medals—Los Angeles in 1984 and Seoul in 1988. Kiraly's 136 Open beach tournament victories place him only three wins behind the all-time leader, Sinjin Smith. With his sites set on the Sydney Olympics in 2000, he seeks to make Olympic history—four gold medals over sixteen years. A devoted father, Kiraly spends most of his free time with his two young sons, Kristian and Kory, and his wife, Janna.

Byron Shewman currently lives in San Diego where he is a writer. Over a long volleyball career, Shewman played on the USA Men's Team between 1971 and 1975. He also played and coached in Spain and France during the late 1970s.

While living abroad for several years, Shewman worked on documentary films and continues to write poetry and fiction. In 1995 Shewman founded, and now directs, Starlings Volleyball Clubs, USA—a national sports program for economically disadvantaged girls. Shewman has written extensively about the sport of volleyball. He authored *Volleyball Centennial: The First 100 Years* (Masters Press, 1995), and recently co-authored a skills text with Karch Kiraly titled *Beach Volleyball* (Human Kinetics, 1999). Currently he is Contributing Editor of *Volleyball Magazine* and is completing a novel.